Contents

Acknowledgements

My special debt is to Sue for her unwavering patience in deciphering my dreadful handwriting and for her inestimable support in helping me through this project at a time when changes were occurring thick and fast. My appreciation also to Peter Pumfrey for his perceptive comments and sustaining advice.

I am very grateful to John Swallow for permission to use extracts from Ongar Comprehensive management and curriculum development materials in addition to the NAHT 14–18 curriculum development proposals.

Thanks are also given to the Inner London Education Authority for permission to use material from D. Hargreaves *Improving Secondary Schools* (1984) p. 2; Longman publishers for permission to use material from B. Goacher *Recording Achievement at 16+* (1987), pp. 61–3; Heinemann Educational Books Ltd for permission to use material from M. Marland (ed.) *Pastoral Care* (1974) p. 75.

It goes without saying that the biggest debt is to those youngsters and staff on whose school experiences this book is based.

Foreword: Towards education for all

This series aims to support teachers as they respond to the challenge they face in meeting the needs of all children in their school, particularly those identified as having special educational needs.

Although there have been many useful publications in the field of special educational needs during the last decade, the distinguishing feature of the present series of volumes lies in their concern with specific areas of the curriculum in primary and secondary schools. We have tried to produce a series of conceptually coherent and professionally relevant books, each of which is concerned with ways in which children with varying levels of ability and motivation can be taught together. The books draw on the experience of practising teachers, teacher trainers and researchers and seek to provide practical guidelines on ways in which specific areas of the curriculum can be made more accessible to all children. The volumes provide many examples of curriculum adaptation, classroom activities, teacher–child interactions, as well as the mobilisation of resources inside and outside the school.

The series is organised largely in terms of age and subject groupings, but three 'overview' volumes have been prepared in order to provide an account of some major current issues and developments. Seamus Hegarty's *Meeting Special Needs in Ordinary Schools* gives an introduction to the field of special needs as a whole, whilst Sheila Wolfendale's *Primary Schools and Special Needs* and John Sayer's *Secondary Schools for All?* address issues more specifically concerned with primary and secondary schools respectively. We hope that curriculum specialists will find essential background and contextual material in these overview volumes.

In addition, a section of this series will be concerned with examples of obstacles to learning. All of these specific special needs can be seen on a continuum ranging from mild to severe, or from temporary and transient to long-standing or permanent. These include difficulties in learning or in adjustment and behaviour, as well as problems resulting largely from sensory or physical impairments or from difficulties of communication from whatever cause. We hope that teachers will consult the volumes in this section for guidance on working with children with specific difficulties.

The series aims to make a modest 'distance learning' contribution to meeting the needs of teachers working with the whole range of pupils with special educational needs by offering a set of resource materials relating to specific areas of the primary and secondary curriculum and by suggesting ways in which learning obstacles, whatever their origin, can be identified and addressed.

We hope that these materials will not only be used for private study but be subjected to critical scrutiny by school-based inservice groups sharing common curricular interests and by staff of institutions of higher education concerned with both special needs teaching and specific curriculum areas. The series has been planned to provide a resource for Local Education Authority (LEA) advisers, specialist teachers from all sectors of the education service, educational psychologists, and teacher working parties. We hope that the books will provide a stimulus for dialogue and serve as catalysts for improved practice.

It is our hope that parents will also be encouraged to read about new ideas in teaching children with special needs so that they can be in a better position to work in partnership with teachers on the basis of an informed and critical understanding of current difficulties and developments. The goal of 'Education for All' can only be reached if we succeed in developing a working partnership between teachers, pupils, parents, and the community at large.

ELEMENTS OF A WHOLE-SCHOOL APPROACH

Meeting special educational needs in ordinary schools is much more than a process of opening school doors to admit children previously placed in special schools. It involves a radical re-examination of what all schools have to offer all children. Our efforts will be judged in the long term by our success with children who are already in ordinary schools but whose needs are not being met, for whatever reason.

The additional challenge of achieving full educational as well as social integration for children now in special schools needs to be seen in the wider context of a major reappraisal of what ordinary schools have to offer the pupils already in them. The debate about integration of handicapped and disabled children in ordinary schools should not be allowed to overshadow the movement for curriculum reform in the schools themselves. If successful, this could promote the fuller integration of the children already in the schools.

If this is the aim of current policy, as it is of this series of unit texts, we have to begin by examining ways in which schools and school policies can themselves be a major element in children's difficulties.

Can schools cause special needs?

Traditionally, we have looked for causes of learning difficulty in the child. Children have been subjected to tests and investigations by doctors, psychologists and teachers with the aim of pinpointing the nature of the problem and in the hope that this might lead to specific programmes of teaching and intervention. We less frequently ask ourselves whether what and how we teach and the way in which we organise and manage our schools could themselves be a major cause of children's difficulties.

The shift of emphasis towards a whole-school policy is sometimes described in terms of a move away from the deficit or medical model of special education towards a more environmental or ecological model. Clearly, we are concerned here with an interaction between the two. No one would deny that the origins of some learning difficulties do lie in the child. But even where a clear cause can be established – for example, a child with severe brain damage, or one with a serious sensory or motor disorder – it would be simplistic to attribute all the child's learning difficulties to the basic impairment alone.

The ecological model starts from the position that the growth and development of children can be understood only in relation to the nature of their interactions with the various environments which impinge on them and with which they are constantly interacting. These environments include the home and each individual member of the immediate and extended family. Equally important are other children in the neighbourhood and at school, as well as people with whom the child comes into casual or closer contact. We also need to consider the local and wider community and its various institutions – not least, the powerful influence of television, which for some children represents more hours of information intake than is provided by teachers during eleven years of compulsory education. The ecological model thus describes a gradually widening series of concentric circles, each of which provides a powerful series of influences and possibilities for interaction – and therefore learning.

Schools and schooling are only one of many environmental influences affecting the development and learning of children. A great deal has been learned from other environments before the child enters school and much more will be learned after the child leaves full-time education. Schools represent a relatively powerful series of environments, not all concerned with formal learning. During the hours spent in school, it is hard to estimate the extent to which the number and nature of the interactions experienced by any one child are directly concerned with formal teaching and learning. Social interactions with other children also need to be considered.

Questions concerned with access to the curriculum lie at the heart of any whole-school policy. What factors limit the access of certain children to the curriculum? What modifications are necessary to ensure fuller curriculum access? Are there areas of the curriculum from which some children are excluded? Is this because they are thought 'unlikely to be able to benefit'? And even if they are physically present, are there particular lessons or activities which are inaccessible because textbooks or worksheets demand a level of literacy and comprehension which effectively prevent access? Are there tasks in which children partly or wholly fail to understand the language which the teacher is using? Are some teaching styles inappropriate for individual children?

Is it possible that some learning difficulties arise from the ways in which schools are organised and managed? For example, what messages are we conveying when we separate some children from others? How does the language we use to describe certain children reflect our own values and assumptions? How do schools transmit value judgements about children who succeed and those who do not? In the days when there was talk of comprehensive schools being 'grammar schools for all', what hope was there for children who were experiencing significant learning difficulties? And even today, what messages are we transmitting to children and their peers when we exclude them from participation in some school activities? How many children with special needs will be entered for the new General Certificate of Secondary Education (GCSE) examinations? How many have taken or will take part in Technical and Vocational Education Initiative (TVEI) schemes?

The argument here is not that all children should have access to all aspects of the curriculum. Rather it is a plea for the individualisation of learning opportunities for all children. This requires a broad curriculum with a rich choice of learning opportunities designed to suit the very wide range of individual needs.

Curriculum reform

The last decade has seen an increasingly interventionist approach by Her Majesty's Inspectors of Education (HMI), by officials of the Department of Education and Science (DES) and by individual Secretaries of State. The 'Great Debate', allegedly beginning in 1976, led to a flood of curriculum guidelines from the centre. The garden is secret no longer. Whilst Britain is far from the centrally imposed curriculum found in some other countries, government is increasingly insisting that schools must reflect certain key areas of experience for all pupils, and in particular those concerned with the world of work (*sic*), with science and technology, and with economic awareness. These priorities are also reflected in the prescriptions for teacher education laid down with an increasing degree of firmness from the centre.

There are indications that a major reappraisal of curriculum content and access is already under way and seems to be well supported by teachers. Perhaps the best known and most recent examples can be found in the series of Inner London Education Authority (ILEA) reports concerned with secondary, primary and special education, known as the Hargreaves, Thomas and Fish Reports (ILEA, 1984, 1985a, 1985b). In particular, the Hargreaves Report envisaged a radical reform of the secondary curriculum, based to some extent on his book *Challenge for the Comprehensive School* (Hargreaves, 1982). This envisages a major shift of emphasis from the 'cognitive–academic' curriculum of many secondary schools towards one emphasising more personal involvement by pupils in selecting their own patterns of study from a wider range of choice. If the proposals in these reports were to be even partially implemented, pupils with special needs would stand to benefit from such a wholesale review of the curriculum of the school as a whole.

Pupils with special needs also stand to benefit from other developments in mainstream education. These include new approaches to records of achievement, particularly 'profiling' and a greater emphasis on criterion–referenced assessment. Some caution has already been expressed about the extent to which the new GCSE examinations will reach less able children previously excluded from the Certificate of Secondary Education. Similar caution is justified in relation to the TVEI and the Certificate of Pre-Vocational Education (CPVE). And what about the new training initiatives for school leavers and the 14–19 age group in general? Certainly, the pronouncements of the Manpower Services Commission (MSC) emphasise a policy of provision for all, and have made specific arrangements for young people with special needs, including those with disabilities. In the last analysis, society and its institutions will be judged by their success in preparing the majority of young people to make an effective and valued contribution to the community as a whole.

A CLIMATE OF CHANGE

Despite the very real and sometimes overwhelming difficulties faced by schools and teachers as a result of underfunding and professional unrest, there are encouraging signs of change and reform which, if successful, could have a significant impact not only on children with special needs but on all children. Some of these are briefly mentioned below.

The campaign for equal opportunities

First, we are more aware of the need to confront issues concerned with civil rights and equal opportunities. All professionals concerned with human services are being asked to examine their own attitudes and practices and to question the extent to which these might unwittingly or even deliberately discriminate unfairly against some sections of the population.

We are more conscious than ever of the need to take positive steps to promote the full access of girls and women not only to full educational opportunities but also to the whole range of community resources and services, including employment, leisure, housing, social security and the right to property. We have a similar concern for members of ethnic and religious groups who have been and still are victims of discrimination and restricted opportunities for participation in society and its institutions. It is no accident that the title of the Swann Report on children from ethnic minorities was *Education for All* (Committee of Inquiry, 1985). This too is the theme of the present series and the underlying aim of the movement to meet the whole range of special needs in ordinary schools.

The equal opportunities movement has not itself always fully accepted people with disabilities and special needs. At national level, there is no legislation specifically concerned with discrimination against people with disabilities, though this does exist in some other countries. The Equal Opportunities Commission does not concern itself with disability issues. On the other hand, an increasing number of local authorities and large corporations claim to be 'Equal Opportunities Employers', specifically mentioning disability alongside gender, ethnicity and sexual orientation. Furthermore, the 1986 Disabled Persons Act, arising from a private member's Bill and now on the statute book, seeks to carry forward for adults some of the more positive features of the 1981 Education Act – for example, it provides for the rights of all people with disabilities to take part or be represented in discussion and decision-making concerning services provided for them.

These developments, however, have been largely concerned with children or adults with disabilities, rather than with children already in ordinary schools. Powerful voluntary organisations such as MENCAP (the Royal Society for Mentally Handicapped Children and Adults) and the Spastics Society have helped to raise political and public awareness of the needs of children with disabilities and have fought hard and on the whole successfully to secure better services for them and for their families. Similarly, organisations of adults with disabilities, such as the British Council of Organisations for Disabled People, are pressing hard for better quality, integrated education, given their own personal experiences of segregated provision.

Special needs and social disadvantage

Even these developments have largely bypassed two of the largest groups now in special schools: those with moderate learning difficulties and those with emotional and behavioural difficulties. There are no powerful pressure groups to speak for them, for the same reason that no pressure groups speak for the needs of children with special needs already in ordinary schools. Many of these children come from families which do not readily form themselves into associations and pressure groups. Many of their parents are unemployed, on low incomes or dependent on social security; many live in overcrowded conditions in poor quality housing or have long-standing health problems. Some members of these families have themselves experienced school failure and rejection as children.

Problems of poverty and disadvantage are common in families of children with special needs already in ordinary schools. Low achievement and social disadvantage are clearly associated, though it is important not to assume that there is a simple relation between them. Although most children from socially disadvantaged backgrounds have not been identified as low achieving, there is still a high correlation between social-class membership and educational achievement, with middle-class children distancing themselves increasingly in educational achievements and perhaps also socially from children from working-class backgrounds – another form of segregation within what purports to be the mainstream.

The probability of socially disadvantaged children being identified as having special needs is very much greater than in other children. An early estimate suggested that it was more than seven times as high, when social disadvantage was defined by the presence of all three of the following indices: overcrowding (more than 1.5 persons per room), low income (supplementary benefit or free school meals) and adverse family circumstances (coming from a single-parent home or a home with more than five children) (Wedge and Prosser, 1973). Since this study was published, the number of families coming into these categories has greatly increased as a result of deteriorating economic conditions and changing social circumstances.

In this wider sense, the problem of special needs is largely a problem of social disadvantage and poverty. Children with special needs are therefore doubly vulnerable to underestimation of their abilities: first, because of their family and social backgrounds, and second, because of their low achievements. A recent large-scale study of special needs provision in junior schools suggests that while teachers' attitudes to low-achieving children are broadly positive, they are pessimistic about the ability of such children to derive much benefit from increased special needs provision (Croll and Moses, 1985).

Partnership with parents

The Croll and Moses survey of junior school practice confirms that teachers still tend to attribute many children's difficulties to adverse home circumstances. How many times have we heard comments along the lines of 'What can you expect from a child from that kind of family?' Is this not a form of stereotyping at least as damaging as racist and sexist attitudes?

Partnership with parents of socially disadvantaged children thus presents a very different challenge from that portrayed in the many reports of successful practice in some special schools. Nevertheless, the challenge can be and is being met. Paul Widlake's recent books (1984, 1985) give the lie to the oft-expressed view that some parents are 'not interested in their child's education'. Widlake documents project after project in which teachers and parents have worked well together. Many of these projects have involved teachers visiting homes rather than parents attending school meetings. There is also now ample research to show that children whose parents listen to them reading at home tend to read better and to enjoy reading more than other children (Topping and Wolfendale, 1985; see also Sheila Wolfendale's *Primary Schools and Special Needs*, in the present series).

Support in the classroom

If teachers in ordinary schools are to identify and meet the whole range of special needs, including those of children currently in special schools, they are entitled to support. Above all, this must come from the head teacher and from the senior staff of the school; from any special needs specialists or teams already in the school; from members of the new advisory and support services, as well as from educational psychologists, social workers and any health professionals who may be involved.

This support can take many forms. In the past, support meant removing the child for considerable periods of time into the care of remedial teachers either within the school or coming from outside. Withdrawal now tends to be discouraged, partly because it is thought to be another form of segregation within the ordinary school, and therefore in danger of isolating and stigmatising children, and partly because it deprives children of access to lessons and activities available to other children. In a major survey of special needs provision in middle and secondary schools, Clunies-Ross and Wimhurst (1983) showed that children with special needs were most often withdrawn from science and modern languages in order to find the time to give them extra help with literacy.

Many schools and LEAs are exploring ways in which both teachers and children can be supported without withdrawing children from ordinary classes. For example, special needs teachers increasingly are working alongside their colleagues in ordinary classrooms, not just with a small group of children with special needs but also with all children. Others are working as consultants to their colleagues in discussing the level of difficulty demanded of children following a particular course or specific lesson. An account of recent developments in consultancy is given in Hanko (1985), with particular reference to children with difficulties of behaviour or adjustment.

Although traditional remedial education is undergoing radical reform, major problems remain. Implementation of new approaches is uneven both between and within LEAs. Many schools still have a remedial department or are visited by peripatetic remedial teachers who withdraw children for extra tuition in reading with little time for consultation with school staff. Withdrawal is still the preferred mode of providing extra help in primary schools, as suggested in surveys of current practice (Clunies-Ross and Wimhurst, 1983; Hodgson, Clunies-Ross and Hegarty, 1984; Croll and Moses, 1985).

Nevertheless, an increasing number of schools now see withdrawal as only one of a widening range of options, only to be used where the child's individually assessed needs suggest that this is indeed the most appropriate form of provision. Other alternatives are now being considered. The overall aim of most of these involves the development of a working partnership between the ordinary class teacher and members of teams with particular responsibility for meeting special needs. This partnership can take a variety of forms, depending on particular circumstances and individual preferences. Much depends on the sheer credibility of special needs teachers, their perceived capacity to offer support and advice and, where necessary, direct, practical help.

We can think of the presence of the specialist teacher as being on a continuum of visibility. A 'high-profile' specialist may sit alongside a pupil with special needs, providing direct assistance and support in participating in activities being followed by the rest of the class. A 'low-profile' specialist may join with a colleague in what is in effect a team-teaching situation, perhaps spending a little more time with individuals or groups with special needs. An even lower profile is provided by teachers who may not set foot in the classroom at all but who may spend considerable periods of time in discussion with colleagues on ways in which the curriculum can be made more accessible to all children in the class, including the least able. Such discussions may involve an examination of textbooks and other reading assignments for readability, conceptual difficulty and relevance of content, as well as issues concerned with the presentation of the material, language modes and complexity used to explain what is required, and the use of different approaches to teacher-pupil dialogue.

IMPLICATIONS FOR TEACHER TRAINING

Issues of training are raised by the authors of the three overview works in this series but permeate all the volumes concerned with specific areas of the curriculum or specific areas of special needs.

The scale and complexity of changes taking place in the field of special needs and the necessary transformation of the teacher-training curriculum imply an agenda for teacher training that is nothing less than retraining and supporting every teacher in the country in working with pupils with special needs.

Although teacher training represented one of the three major priorities identified by the Warnock Committee, the resources devoted to this priority have been meagre, despite a strong commitment to training from teachers,

LEAs, staff of higher education, HMI and the DES itself. Nevertheless, some positive developments can be noted (for more detailed accounts of developments in teacher education see Sayer and Jones, 1985 and Robson, Sebba, Mittler and Davies, 1988).

Initial training

At the initial training level, we now find an insistence that all teachers in training must be exposed to a compulsory component concerned with meeting special needs in the ordinary school. The Council for the Accreditation of Teacher Education (CATE) and HMI seem set to enforce these criteria; institutions that do not meet them will not be accredited for teacher training.

Although this policy is welcome from a special needs perspective, many questions remain. Where will the staff to teach these courses come from? What happened to the Warnock recommendations for each teacher-training institution to have a small team of staff specifically concerned with this area? Even when a team exists, they can succeed in 'permeating' a special needs element into initial teacher training only to the extent that they influence all their fellow specialist tutors to widen their teaching perspectives to include children with special needs.

Special needs departments in higher education face similar problems to those confronting special needs teams in secondary schools. They need to gain access to and influence the work of the whole institution. They also need to avoid the situation where the very existence of an active special needs department results in colleagues regarding special needs as someone else's responsibility, not theirs.

Despite these problems, the outlook in the long term is favourable. More and more teachers in training are at least receiving an introduction to special needs; are being encouraged to seek out information on special needs policy and practice in the schools in which they are doing their teaching practice, and are being introduced to a variety of approaches to meeting their needs. Teaching materials are being prepared specifically for initial teacher-training students. Teacher trainers have also been greatly encouraged by the obvious interest and commitment of students to children with special needs; optional and elective courses on this subject have always been over-subscribed.

Inservice courses for designated teachers

Since 1983, the government has funded a series of one-term full-time courses in polytechnics and universities to provide intensive training for designated teachers with specific responsibility for pupils with special needs in ordinary schools (see *Meeting Special Needs in Ordinary Schools* by Seamus Hegarty in this series for information on research on evaluation of their effectiveness). These courses are innovative in a number of respects. They bring LEA and higher-education staff together in a productive working partnership. The seconded teacher, headteacher, LEA adviser and higher-education tutor enter into a commitment to train and support the teachers in becoming change agents in their own schools. Students spend two days a week in their own schools initiating and implementing change. All teachers with designated responsibilities for pupils with special needs have the right to be considered for these one-term courses, which are now a national priority area for which central funding is available. However, not all teachers can gain access to these courses as the institutions are geographically very unevenly distributed.

Other inservice courses

The future of inservice education for teachers (INSET) in education in general and special needs in particular is in a state of transition. Since April 1987, the government has abolished the central pooling arrangements which previously funded courses and has replaced these by a system in which LEAs are required to identify their training requirements and to submit these to the DES for funding. LEAs are being asked to negotiate training needs with each school as part of a policy of staff development and appraisal. Special needs is one of nineteen national priority areas that will receive 70 per cent funding from the DES, as is training for further education (FE) staff with special needs responsibilities.

These new arrangements, known as Grant Related Inservice Training (GRIST), will change the face of inservice training for all teachers but time is needed to assess their impact on training opportunities and teacher effectiveness (see Mittler, 1986, for an interim account of the implications of the proposed changes). In the meantime, there is serious concern about the future of secondments for courses longer than one term. Additional staffing will also be needed in higher education to respond to the wider range of demand.

An increasing number of 'teaching packages' have become available for teachers working with pupils with special needs. Some (though not all) of these are well designed and evaluated. Most of them are school-based and can be used by small groups of teachers working under the supervision of a trained tutor.

The best known of these is the Special Needs Action Programme (SNAP) originally developed for Coventry primary schools (Muncey and Ainscow, 1982) but now being adapted for secondary schools. This is based on a form of pyramid training in which co-ordinators from each school are trained to train colleagues in their own school or sometimes in a consortium of local schools. Evaluation by a National Foundation for Educational Research (NFER) research team suggests that SNAP is potentially an effective approach to school-based inservice training, providing that strong management support is guaranteed by the headteacher and by senior LEA staff (see Hegarty, *Meeting Special Needs in Ordinary Schools*, this series, for a brief summary).

Does training work?

Many readers of this series of books are likely to have recent experience of training courses. How many of them led to changes in classroom practice? How often have teachers been frustrated by their inability to introduce and implement change in their schools on returning from a course? How many heads actively support their staff in becoming change agents? How many teachers returning from advanced one-year courses have experienced 'the re-entry phenomenon'? At worst, this is quite simply being ignored: neither the LEA adviser, nor the head nor any one else asks about special interests and skills developed on the course and how these could be most effectively put to good use in the school. Instead, the returning member of staff is put through various re-initiation rituals ('Enjoyed your holiday?'), or is given responsibilities bearing no relation to interests developed on the course. Not infrequently, colleagues with less experience and fewer qualifications are promoted over their heads during their absence.

At a time of major initiatives in training, it may seem churlish to raise questions about the effectiveness of staff training. It is necessary to do so because training resources are limited and because the morale and motivation of the teaching force depend on satisfaction with what is offered – indeed, on opportunities to negotiate what is available with course providers. Blind faith in training for training's sake soon leads to disillusionment and frustration.

For the last three years, a team of researchers at Manchester University and Huddersfield Polytechnic have been involved in a DES funded project which aimed to assess the impact of a range of inservice courses on teachers working with pupils with special educational needs (see Robson, Sebba, Mittler and Davies, 1988, for a full account and Sebba, 1987, for a briefer interim report). A variety of courses was evaluated; some were held for one evening a week for a term; others were one-week full time; some were award-bearing, others were not. The former included the North-West regional diploma in special needs, the first example of a course developed in total partnership between a university and a polytechnic which allowed students to take modules from either institution and also gave credit recognition to specific Open University and LEA courses. The research also evaluated the effectiveness of an already published and disseminated course on behavioural methods of teaching – the EDY course (Farrell, 1985).

Whether or not the readers of these books are or will be experiencing a training course, or whether their training consists only of the reading of one or more of the books in this series, it may be useful to conclude by highlighting a number of challenges facing teachers and teacher trainers in the coming decades.

1. We are all out of date in relation to the challenges that we face in our work.
2. Training in isolation achieves very little. Training must be seen as part of a wider programme of change and development of the institution as a whole.
3. Each LEA, each school and each agency needs to develop a strategic approach to staff development, involving detailed identification of training and development needs with the staff as a whole and with each individual member of staff.
4. There must be a commitment by management to enable the staff member to try to implement ideas and methods learned on the course.
5. This implies a corresponding commitment by the training institutions to prepare the student to become an agent of change.

6. There is more to training than attending courses. Much can be learned simply by visiting other schools, seeing teachers and other professionals at work in different settings and exchanging ideas and experiences. Many valuable training experiences can be arranged within a single school or agency, or by a group of teachers from different schools meeting regularly to carry out an agreed task.
7. There is now no shortage of books, periodicals, videos and audio-visual aids concerned with the field of special needs. Every school should therefore have a small staff library which can be used as a resource by staff and parents. We hope that the present series of unit texts will make a useful contribution to such a library.

The publishers and I would like to thank the many people – too numerous to mention – who have helped to create this series. In particular we would like to thank the Associate Editors, James Hogg, Peter Pumfrey, Tessa Roberts and Colin Robson, for their active advice and guidance; the Honorary Advisory Board, Neville Bennett, Marion Blythman, George Cooke, John Fish, Ken Jones, Sylvia Phillips, Klaus Wedell and Phillip Williams, for their comments and suggestion; and the teachers, teacher trainers and special needs advisers who took part in our information surveys.

Professor Peter Mittler   University of Manchester
                                            January 1987

REFERENCES

Clunies-Ross, L. and Wimhurst, S. (1983) *The Right Balance: Provision for Slow Learners in Secondary Schools.* Windsor: NFER/Nelson.
Committee of Inquiry (1985) *Education for All.* London: HMSO (The Swann Report).
Croll, P. and Moses, D. (1985) *One in Five: The Assessment and Incidence of Special Educational Needs.* London: Routledge & Kegan Paul.
Farrell, P. (ed.) (1985) *EDY: Its Impact on Staff Training in Mental Handicap.* Manchester: Manchester University Press.
Hanko, G. (1985) *Special Needs in Ordinary Classrooms: An Approach to Teacher Support and Pupil Care in Primary and Secondary Schools.* Oxford: Blackwell.
Hargreaves, D. (1982) *Challenge for the Comprehensive School.* London: Routledge & Kegan Paul.
Hodgson, A., Clunies-Ross, L. and Hegarty, S. (1984) *Learning Together.* Windsor: NFER/Nelson.
Inner London Education Authority (1984) *Improving Secondary Education.* London: ILEA (The Hargreaves Report).
Inner London Education Authority (1985a) *Improving Primary Schools.* London: ILEA (The Thomas Report).
Inner London Education Authority (1985b) *Equal Opportunities for All?* London: ILEA (The Fish Report).
Mittler, P. (1986) The new look in inservice training. *British Journal of Special Education*, **13**, pp. 50–51.
Muncey, J. and Ainscow, M. (1982) Launching SNAP in Coventry. *Special Education: Forward Trends*, **10**, pp. 3–5.
Robson, C., Sebba, J., Mittler, P. and Davies, G. (1988) *Inservice Training and Special*

Needs: Running Short School-Focused Courses. Manchester: Manchester University Press.

Sayer, J. and Jones, N. (eds) (1985) *Teacher Training and Special Educational Needs.* Beckenham: Croom Helm.

Sebba, J. (1987) The development of short, school-focused INSET courses in special educational needs. *Research Papers in Education,* **2,** 1–29.

Topping, K. and Wolfendale, S. (eds) (1985) *Parental Involvement in Children's Reading.* Beckenham: Croom Helm.

Wedge, P. and Prosser, H. (1973) *Born to Fail?* London: National Children's Bureau.

Widlake, P. (1984) *How to Reach the Hard to Teach.* Milton Keynes: Open University Press.

Widlake, P. (1985) *Reducing Educational Disadvantage.* London: Routledge & Kegan Paul.

Preface

This volume is shaped by a conviction that the pastoral curriculum can form the essence of a whole-school approach to the needs of adolescents both in and, consequently, beyond school. The book is organised into four parts. We start by considering issues which surround the term 'whole-school approaches' to needs, and within this exploration the concept of special education is introduced.

The process of defining needs is influenced by attitudes. Definitions of educational needs are therefore resisted. Instead, illuminative descriptions are given of youngsters seen in the context of the school environment. In this way it is hoped that the reader will be able to identify with and reach a greater understanding of some of the causal factors of needs within the secondary-school situation.

Part Two introduces the developing concept of pastoral care. It is conjectured that the status and effectiveness of pastoral care, as a distinct and positive whole-school response to adolescent needs, is influenced by its placement in the curriculum. In numerous schools pastoral care has operated from the periphery of the curriculum whereby it has been used either as a punitive or as a first-aid response to crisis. There are distinct opportunities, particularly within current 14–19 initiatives, for pastoral care to assume a centralised position within the curriculum. This core placement will have an enormous and innovative impact upon the quality of learning across the whole curriculum for all youngsters.

Part Three examines in detail those processes which lie at the heart of the pastoral curriculum. It is emphasised that the creation of well-defined learning climates and of counselling and problem-solving, identification, assessment and recording of achievements, are positive tutoring processes which could extend and develop the role of the teacher-facilitator within the whole-school curriculum. This part of the volume concludes by introducing a case study which illustrates how these pastoral processes shaped the curriculum experiences of a group of 14 and 15 year olds.

Part Four raises the issue of staff development. It is stressed that a whole-school approach to needs should incorporate considerations about staff needs, with pastoral processes extending to all personnel within the school. The book concludes with detailed staff development activities which encourage reflective consideration of some of the issues raised in each chapter of the book.

Within a book which implicitly assumes equal regard for all there is no deliberate distinction made between the sexes. References to either sex are therefore used indiscriminately.

I must make it clear that the views expressed in this book are my own. They do not necessarily reflect those of my present employer or any other people with whom I have worked over the years. The case studies and comments, whilst drawn from an amalgam of real situations, have been extensively modified in order that identifying details can be omitted. It is entirely coincidental if they bear any resemblance to any person or situation.

Part One   The developing concept of special educational need

This part introduces the all-pervasive concept of special educational needs within adolescence.

Special educational needs and the school leaver: the widening concept

The purposes of this chapter are to consider:

- the issue of a whole-school approach to special educational needs
- the interrelated processes of adolescent development and special educational needs
- four aspects of achievement
- five adolescents who exhibit distinct developmental needs.

WHOLE-SCHOOL APPROACHES TO MEETING SPECIAL NEEDS

A whole-school response to needs necessitates a shared responsibility for the educational development of youngsters. This shared responsibility demands that all staff and youngsters within the school respond to perceived and articulated developmental needs.

Sayer, in the introductory book to this series comments, 'It is not a specialised volume for special educators, although it makes demands on them to share in forming a broader context in which their work is part of everyone's concern' Sayer (1987).

This 'broader context' takes special needs' provision outside the confines of the special unit, the remedial class, the withdrawal group, the sanctuary or, as I have encountered, the Alternative Curriculum Enterprise (ACE) group. A broader concept is about a whole-school policy which in practical terms means that all staff are involved in meeting educational needs as they arise within the learning situation.

WHOLE-SCHOOL APPROACHES AND INTEGRATION

Integration is at the root of any discussions about whole-school approaches to special educational needs. One member of staff at a recent staff-development conference exclaimed that she could not accept the term 'integration' because it conveyed distinct impressions about the people who were being integrated. They were the people being received and having 'good done to them'. If the term 'desegregation' were to be used rather than 'integration' there is an implication that barriers are being broken down, that groups are unified into a common whole. Within this common whole a wider definition of need and provision is made. All individuals are viewed as having distinct and evolving needs which demand a whole-school management and curriculum approach.

It is really not sufficient and is blatantly dishonest to pander to notions of integration by merely performing a selection of cosmetic exercises. Over many years I have observed numerous practices which are totally inconsistent with often well-documented school policies. Perhaps readers can identify with them:

- the renaming of 'remedial department' as 'special resources department', even though most youngsters in the department still take most of their lessons in a separate and isolated unit;
- the inclusion of the 'alternative curriculum' slot on the option form because special-needs (or so-called 'remedial') youngsters cannot cope with the demands of the other option choices;
- students whose upper-school curriculum is predominantly made up of 'practical' and so-called 'less academic' subjects;
- heads of special-education departments receiving much lower allowance for curriculum responsibilities than other colleagues;
- heads of special-education departments having to wait until the timetable has been finished before they are allowed on a very *ad hoc* basis to mop up the spare slots for work 'across the curriculum';
- special-education departments not being represented at middle management or curriculum development meetings.

One school which professed a whole-school approach to special educational needs had centred its 'Special Needs Resource Unit' within the main school; originally the old remedial department was run from the Nissen hut at the end of the playground. Its new placement was in line with the integrative nature of the well-documented whole-school policy. Ironically the youngsters were, for 70 per cent of their timetables, offered 'alternative curricula' within the resource unit. They felt different, inferior: 'exposed', as one youngster put it. They would hang around at the end of lessons, some with heads under their desks, until the next mainstream lesson had started. Then they would leave the unit. They had acutely low levels of self-esteem, essentially because, although the head of unit valued them, the wider school community projected very negative messages back to them both through the ways in which it was organised and the attitudes which permeated this organisation.

Whilst a number of schools still retain units and resource centres, their apparent main focus is now to resource mainstream learning activities. Support across the curriculum however is implemented in a variety of ways. A recurring feature is for a support teacher to accompany a youngster into mainstream lessons to help him with the basics of reading and writing. Whilst there is a nominal gesture towards integration, the youngster and the support teacher are often still isolated because neither of them are officially drawn into the main body of the lesson. Whereas previously the youngster was on the curriculum periphery, isolated within the remedial unit, he is still receiving a peripheral educative experience, now, ironically, within mainstream lessons.

There is a degree of anxiety amongst some secondary staff about having other adults in the classroom with them. Secondary teachers are still regularly seen as subject experts who are expected to teach their subject efficiently. To have another person in the classroom, as one teacher recently retorted, 'is to have an added distraction'. In the context of mainstream support for special needs, this 'added distraction', the support teacher, feels equally anxious because he is unsure of his role within the classroom.

The process of mainstream support demands a reclarification of roles, tasks and procedures in the classroom which has implications for the teacher, the supporter and the taught.

Whole approaches to special education, whether at the wider school or classroom level, involve a concept of education which in its essence encourages reciprocal support for all within the classroom situation. Whilst it could be argued that the case study in Chapter 8 emphasises an isolationist approach to special education, our concern was to illustrate to staff that the approaches used to meet a wide variety of needs present in the group were school approaches which were universal in their application. These universal processes lie at the heart of Part Three of this volume. Sue Johnson's case study, which concludes Part Three, vividly illustrates these processes in practice.

Sayer (1987) expounds, 'Non-segregation is a nonsense if it is only about children with special educational needs. It has to be about the needs of the whole population, resourced as a whole and resourcing each other.' An approach which encourages desegregation ensures that the providers and the provided are involved in mutually supportive development.

DEFINING SPECIAL EDUCATIONAL NEEDS

Special educational needs is a term fraught with ambiguity and professional controversy. The Warnock Report claims that one in five youngsters will at some time during their school career have special educational needs (Warnock Report, 1978). Ten years after Warnock and with a rapidly changing social and economic climate, which places increasing demands on developing adolescents, one has to ask: why stop at 20 per cent? Indeed it appears grossly inappropriate even to contemplate percentage figures when addressing the increasingly complex concept of special educational needs.

The 1981 Act, which consolidated Warnock, again attempts to tackle the ambiguity surrounding the concept. The Act states 'If a youngster has a "learning difficulty" then special educational provision should be made.' But what do we understand by 'learning difficulties'? In reality ask parents, youngsters and in my experience most teaching staff for their interpretations and the responses cluster around poor literacy and numeracy ability – 'the basics', 'the remedial kids'.

The Warnock Report illuminated a fundamental tautological issue when redefining the concept of special educational needs. This was the importance of moving away from notions of handicap and looking instead at the complexity of individual needs across a wider spectrum of youngsters.

The basic tenet underlying the concept of integration is that developmental needs transcend tight distinct pupil groupings. For example, a cognitively less able child may be socially very mature; on the other hand a physically handicapped youngster may be socially mature and cognitively less able; alternatively a cognitively more able child may be emotionally very retarded. Both the more academically able and those pupils who are less academically able, indeed all pupils, have similar needs.

Our concept of special education has to reach beyond the 'remedial' label which so often, in spite of legislation, is synonymous with the term 'learning difficulties'. The concept of learning difficulties has to include within its parameters those developmental difficulties experienced by adolescents.

E. Erikson provides a comprehensive and logically cohesive 'stage' theory of human development which has immense significance to those people concerned with adolescent development. His fifth stage concentrates upon adolescence and the search for personal identity. Erikson observes that in order to achieve integration of the ego, the young person must 'from all possible and imaginable relations, make a series of ever narrowing selection of personal, occupational, sexual and ideological commitments'. This process involves the young person asking questions about himself in relation to others in his environment so that he can achieve an adequate sense of identity, coupled with the development of satisfactory relations with his peer group. These, in Erikson's assessment, are two of the major developmental tasks at this stage (Erikson, 1968).

Erikson's key issues are those which concern how the adolescent adjusts to the demands contained in:

- personal and social development
- vocational development
- becoming sexually committed
- acquiring values which will shape ideological commitments.

FOUR ASPECTS OF ACHIEVEMENT

Erikson's four key developmental issues are keenly reflected in those four achievement aspects which are introduced at the beginning of the Hargreaves Report (1984). The underlying thrust of this report is that within schools we have to focus upon achievement possibilities and not upon handicap. In its consideration of the secondary curriculum it looks at four aspects of achievement: (see Figure 1.1)

- traditional learning
- practical application of knowledge
- personal and social development
- motivation, commitment and confidence.

This takes the focus of concern away from the underachieving youngster and instead takes a wide overview of achievement aspects. The report emphasises that the 'distinctions are analytical and cannot readily be distinguished within classrooms'.

The range of developmental needs in the secondary school is wide. Given therefore the broad concept of special educational needs, it is perhaps more pertinent to the teacher to resist specific definitions and instead to use illustrations of need observed through the case studies of individual youngsters who are interacting within distinct contexts, and who are attempting to attain achievement at different levels in a range of areas.

ILLUSTRATIONS OF NEED – FIVE YOUNG PEOPLE IN THE SCHOOL ENVIRONMENT

Joe – a confirmation of role

Joe's parents were separated. His mother had custody of him, although he saw his father – with whom he shared an interest in

Figure 1.1   *Four achievement aspects:*

Achievement aspect I

This aspect of achievement is strongly represented in the current 16-plus examinations. It involves most of all the capacity to express oneself in a written form. It requires the capacity to retain propositional knowledge, to select from such knowledge appropriately in response to a specified request, and to do so quickly without reference to possible sources of information. The capacity to memorise and organise material is particularly important. Public examinations measure such achievement in that they are mainly written tests, set with strict time limits and with the requirement that pupils have few or no additional resources available to them. The examinations emphasise knowledge rather than skill; memorisation more than problem-solving or investigational capacities; writing rather than speaking or other forms of communication; speed rather than reflection; individual rather than group achievement.

Achievement aspect II

This aspect of achievement is concerned with the capacity to apply knowledge rather than knowledge itself, with the practical rather than the theoretical, with the oral rather than the written. Problem-solving and investigational skills are more important than the retention of knowledge. This aspect is to some degree measured in public examinations, but it is often seen as secondary and less important than aspect I. It tends to be more difficult, as well as more time-consuming and more expensive, to assess than aspect I.

Achievement aspect III

This aspect is concerned with personal and social skills; the capacity to communicate with others in face-to-face relationships; the ability to co-operate with others in the interests of the group as well as of the individual; initiative, self-reliance and the ability to work without close supervision; and the skills of leadership. This aspect of achievement remains virtually untapped by the 16-plus examinations.

Achievement aspect IV

This aspect of achievement involves motivation and commitment; the willingness to accept failure without destructive consequences; the readiness to preserve; the self-confidence to learn in spite of the difficulty of the task. Such motivation is often regarded as a prerequisite to achievement, rather than as an achievement in itself. We do not deny that motivation is a prerequisite to the other three aspects of achievement, but we also believe that it can be regarded as an achievement in its own right. For some pupils come to their schools without such motivation, yet the school succeeds in generating it in them and, in such circumstances, both the school and the pupils have made an important achievement.

Source: Hargreaves (1984) *Improving Secondary Schools.*

sports-car racing – on a regular basis. Both parents were young and treated Joe very much as a friend. Confidences were exchanged and experiences shared on a very adult level. Within the school situation Joe attempted to relate to staff in this same adult way. However, this potential over-familiarity was often interpreted by staff as insolence. He regularly protested verbally when he thought one of his peers was being unfairly treated. This response was seen as a disruptive one, which it was, in specific situations.

Joe was observed by his head of house over a period of time, in a number of settings. Staff seemed to respond to Joe's behaviour according to how secure they felt in the classroom situation. Those who were sure of their own role in the classroom, who were not afraid to take risks, were prepared to exchange friendly but firm banter with Joe. They were able to come from behind their desks being positive, active participants in the learning process. They were humorous, patient and accepting of Joe. They methodically encouraged him to analyse his own responses to situations, in an attempt to help him mature in a supportive group environment. They attempted to show him that certain forms of behaviour were not appropriate in certain situations. One member of staff encouraged Joe, through the process of role play, to look at the role to which he was adhering. In that situation she was asking him to question himself and to look at himself through the eyes of others. However many staff saw Joe's role as threatening and undermining. In part, this was due to:

- lack of time – 'I have to get through the syllabus.'
- lack of expertise – 'How can you teach people like him in a mixed ability setting?'; and/or
- little knowledge of developmental theories – 'He's disruptive, and that's all there is to it.'

There was a constant confirming of a disruptive role upon him. Salient comments addressed to Joe confirmed this:

'Why do you think you are any different from anyone else?'
'I've heard about you. I make the rules in the classroom, not you!'
'I hear that your mother has been up to school again.' (She had seen the head of house about an administrative matter.)
'I might have guessed it would be you disrupting the group again!'

Joe accepted that he did verbally challenge on many occasions, and he often acted in a clown role. He also made the comment that it was an act and that he was not really 'disruptive'. He saw his behaviour primarily as harmless verbal bantering with adults. In the daily maintenance situation of many a classroom, the response of some staff was understandable. Such interchange was irritating and undermining. The 'costs' to the other students in the group were also a legitimate cause for professional concern.

I am sure many teachers can identify with a situation like the following. It is a typical Friday afternoon. Thirty-plus youngsters have just arrived from a chaotic 'practical' lesson. You have them for last period. You are tired. They are high. You have about half a dozen tasks to administer, and in walks the chief troublemaker. In Joe's case, the immediate response from some staff was to attempt to shut off the source and symptoms of disruption by referring him to the head of house, keeping him in for detention or standing him outside the classroom. Often he would disappear. In the long term this staff response was contributing to the fixation of a role; a role which Joe eventually adopted on a permanent basis.

During his first two years in school he was a happy, humorous, outgoing boy. By his third year he was becoming negatively disruptive, a response that was fixed within the classroom situation. He justified his role behaviour by claiming that 'Staff have it in for me, they are always picking on me, they never look at the good things I do, they don't want me to talk about anything.'

Interestingly, and as is frequently the case, the disruptive role became interfused with the ability role. Eventually Joe's observations were that staff were now calling him 'thick', etc. This fixed role originated from a youngster exhibiting experimental behaviour which many staff, some unwittingly, reinforced and consolidated. The problem was seen solely as Joe, and not the developmental problems he was coping with or the response behaviour from significant people in his environment.

Terry—a disruptive youngster: appropriate/inappropriate curriculum experiences

Terry was 14 and was following a City and Guilds course. In other areas of the curriculum he was designated a 'non-exam' pupil. When he was 7½ years old he was referred to the educational psychologist because, according to the first psychological report, 'He is finding it difficult to keep up in his class.' Such nebulous comments permeated the whole of the report. Even at this early age the focus was upon Terry's having the difficulty. The learning situation from which the difficulties emanated was not examined in detail.

When he was 10 years old he was referred again by his junior school because, according to the psychologist's report, 'Despite help from Mr Smith [remedial teacher] he seems to be failing to make any progress.' His reading age was then 8 years 8 months. A revealing and disturbing development in this second report was the inclusion of the comment, 'Terry is becoming extremely sullen and told me openly he did not like school and did not want to come ... He liked poker.'

It was with this developing open hostility that Terry joined the secondary school. At the age of 13 years he was referred to the educational psychologist for a third time because of 'difficult behaviour' at school. He was now participating in acts of vandalism, as well as becoming violent with those other pupils who often called him 'gypo'. This violence, often verbal and physical, was being directed towards some staff.

Since the age of 7 Terry was well aware of the 'slow learner' label. He was frightened of many situations and tried to bluff his way through such periods. In a closely supervised, contained situation, in control of a tutor/teacher who displayed fairness, Terry often responded in a very positive way. Many problems, however, occurred outside the confines of the tutor/class group when Terry walked around school trying to create an external impression of 'toughness'. His response was that, if a child stared or laughed at him, then he retaliated with violence. He did not have the inner controls to manage this behaviour. There was a contrived effort at image building, and there was a sustained effort to retain this image which gave him 'importance' and self-esteem.

Within a structured situation Terry generally responded positively. He did not lack basic intelligence, but this was often concealed by his immaturity. Violent eruptions of temper and resentment were directed towards those in authority and many of his peers. Under this hard facade there was insecurity which manifested itself in a number of situations:

- When sensitively counselled by his tutor he would uncontrollably cry and project his own feelings of failure on other people.
- When work experience was arranged for him at his request, he refused to go. When counselled, he again expressed feelings of fear about new situations and being on his own, particularly without his quiet and timid friend, Shaun.
- He was looked after by three girls in his group. They would continually try to explain his behaviour and they became his advocates in a number of potentially tense situations. In group situations he would regularly be observed adopting childlike submissive behaviour when in the company of these peer nurture figures.

However, within the curriculum his response to most lessons revealed bored lethargy which, if challenged, often changed to verbal abuse.

A changed response, however, was seen in one curriculum area, a City and Guilds course. Within this course Terry, although occasionally abusive, revealed a mature, self-restrained form of behaviour. One important reason for this rested not only with the content but with the process of curriculum development within the course. The aim of the session was given at the beginning and it was pointed out that everyone had a stake in the responsibility for attaining that aim. Terry therefore knew the reasoning behind certain elements of the course. This did not prevent him from occasionally shouting out that he was 'bored', accompanied by other more explicit expletives, but he felt more involved in the process of his learning. The emphasis was upon developmental group work, whereby Terry was asked to give reasons for, and to reflect upon, how his behaviour affected others and to focus upon his feelings at a period of outburst. Other individuals within the group, including the two adults, were asked to reflect their feelings back to Terry. From this process Terry was able to look at reasons for action and he attempted to modify some inappropriate forms of behaviour. He participated in the group 'coffee rota', and seriously undertook his rota duty by imitating a waiter, with his pad and pencil taking orders – 'coffee, no sugar, milk?', etc. He was actively participating in group work, was seen to be and felt that he was a valued group member.

Interestingly, around school his behaviour was improving in those areas where staff were seen to be fair, and were confident enough in themselves, to allow him to question, and grow. One traditional 'no-nonsense' head of curriculum area, after liaising with the City and Guilds staff, instead of confronting Terry head-on, bantered intelligently and good humouredly with him, and Terry responded positively.

The inappropriate curriculum responses were:

- from those staff who were either over-friendly to the point of almost colluding with him
- vindictive staff who were out to teach him a lesson
- lessons which had little meaning for him, or other pupils. Often he was the champion for the rights of the 'underdog', he would tell the teacher that 'Not only me but Joe, Kate and Wayne – we're all bored!'

A very positive development within an appropriate curriculum area took place when the City and Guilds course held an open day to display the work completed by the youngsters that term. Terry felt sufficiently motivated to compile a display piece on a project about 'break dancing', a piece of work which was designed to show evidence of private study during the term. Terry's parents were unable to attend and so the teachers suggested that his grandmother might like to come. Terry nonchalantly replied that he didn't know whether she could come, or whether he wanted her to come. The teachers said that they would give her a ring and arrange to collect her if that would help. In the weeks leading up to the day Terry kept bringing in tatty bits of paper with addresses, telephone numbers and other information on them and asking if his grandmother had been contacted. When the day arrived and his grandmother was brought into school, Terry's response was one of shock, delight, accompanied by a facade of the usual nonchalance. The open day enabled him to share his success with his grandmother who was a very significant person in his life. It facilitated an unusual positive encounter between the school and the home. It consolidated much of the positive group work which underlined the course. It was a curriculum experience which contributed to a noticeable change in Terry's behaviour, group participation and more importantly, his self-esteem. Unfortunately it was a curriculum area which was peripheral to the general curriculum focus of the school.

Sarah – an emotionally and socially underdeveloped but academically able school leaver

Sarah had, since entering secondary school, always achieved creditable examination and written classwork results. Her ensuing reports reflected her cognitive ability:

> An outstanding student. I am looking forward to seeing her gain excellent examination results.
> Always tries hard, a pleasure to teach.
> Work is excellent in this subject, an example to other pupils.

She was of a thin, drawn appearance and at fifteen she dressed in lace-up shoes, pleated navy skirt and wore a belted navy gaberdine. She was known amongst her peers as 'the swot', and she was the subject of many a practical prank instigated by lower-school pupils. She was quiet and conforming and she regularly gained success in formal examinations. Sarah's elderly parents were pleased with and proud of her school performance.

The time came for her to progress 'naturally' into the sixth form, and her study pattern continued to be that of a fairly isolated individual who buried herself continually in her books. She then made application for university and was provisionally accepted, pending gaining acceptable grades. The crunch came in August when the grades gained were not high enough for university entrance. She refused a polytechnic placement because she viewed it, as did her parents, as being not 'academically' suitable. Her retakes did not yield the required grades. She left school and gained placement in local government. Sarah's career pattern had changed direction and she was bewildered and anxious. This is not an evaluative comment related solely to Sarah's experiences but highlights the tasks faced by all adolescents in moving towards greater independence.

People still use the term 'learning difficulties' to refer to the cognitively less able, even though the concept embraces a much more diffuse range of youngsters. We regularly fail to recognise those able pupils who have emotional, social and study behaviour difficulties. It was within these areas that Sarah was quite retarded. She could not face the thought of leaving the safe 'academic' learning situation and yet even in this situation, she had been underfunctioning. Her poor study skills meant that she could learn some facts off by rote, but, because she could not effectively select reading for revision and make notes for essays, she would wade through masses of irrelevant material. However, feedback within her immediate environment made her believe that she was a successful student. The school had failed her in a number of ways by not:

- encouraging her to look at alternative forms of occupational/ study routes
- encouraging the development of appropriate study skills
- extending its boundaries of what makes a successful student
- encouraging Sarah to work in a 'safe', non-threatening group environment in an attempt to develop her skills of social interaction
- identifying and assessing some of her wider-ranging needs during her early schooling.

Some people are isolates. They have made that choice, and are strong and fulfilled within that role. However, occasionally pupils hide behind an academic guise, when in reality they want to relate positively to other people, but they do not have the skills or the self-confidence to initiate and participate in this process. They are existing within a role which they have not come to terms with, and the school curriculum does not encourage them to work positively through this developmental process.

Barry – sexual identity and adolescence

Barry was a sensitive, caring and academically able boy. Superficially he contrived to be an extrovert. In a group of youngsters he would pose, and talk loudly, but in reality he was quite an isolated individual. His key interest in school was in the drama group. He played parts with some aplomb. In this group he mixed fairly comfortably with the girls and with some of the boys. In the wider school environment he was often in the company of girls and it was observed that he was regularly on the receiving end of taunts from some of the more 'macho' boys.

Many youngsters go through a phase of homosexual development whilst establishing their sexual identity. But it appeared that Barry had become emotionally committed to this phase, and he openly displayed fixed feminine traits. In the world of drama he could develop positively. In the wider school community he found this more difficult. After one long summer holiday Barry returned to school dressed in black punk-style clothing. Gone was the immaculate hairstyle, now replaced with 'superglue' spikes. People were now even more aware of Barry's presence. Most youngsters treated him with a distanced respect, coupled with disbelief. Barry, through a variety of modes of dress, was trying to assert himself. He was possibly attempting to convey to others that 'I accept myself, and I am therefore asserting my individuality in whatever way I can.'

What he did need was the opportunity, within a supportive group classroom environment, to articulate openly his developing needs in ways which would consolidate his own self-worth. Our view of handicap develops through value judgements, and the ensuing perceptions of what is 'normal' and acceptable in given circumstances. The development of an appropriate self-image was crucial for Barry who was continually asking himself, 'What picture do I give to others? Does the feedback which others give me make me want to accept myself?'

From a social point of view the central issue for any child with some form of impairment is his acceptance by other people (Thomas, 1978). We have to ask ourselves, how does the school curriculum contribute to this process?

Staff responded in a number of ways. Some laughed at his strutting pose. Others reflected their own inner prejudices and feelings either by referring to him with dismissive descriptions or by ignoring him. Very few openly talked about this aspect of emotional and social development in their classrooms, even though it is a fact of life and, as such, should be tackled within the curriculum. If adolescence is a period when the youngster is trying to establish a personal identity, then the response of the school should be one which is aware of the sexual-developmental needs of youngsters and one which consequently provides a programme which helps these needs to be articulated and met.

Jim – a cognitively less able pupil: the impact of unemployment

Jim was fourteen. In his third year at secondary school he was 'guided' by the staff to choose those subject areas which had a low prestige and status within school, combined science, general studies and modern studies. Given the constraining influence of the examination-orientated curriculum, staff had little choice but to guide him in this direction. His hidden destination was consequently that of 'non-exam' pupil. Success in the school was synonymous with academic success or sporting prowess. It was consequently exceptionally difficult for staff to encourage Jim to accept positively that, with a reading age of 9, he had an impossible task in achieving creditable, traditional examination results. His one status subject area was English which was based upon continuous assessment. Although he only had a reading age of 9, he thought he had a chance of an examination pass in this subject and consequently he worked hard.

He used to pretend he could read plays out loud and fluently in class, having previously learned the parts off by heart at home, with the help of an elder brother. Within the wider curriculum, small learning difficulties to him were insurmountable. He tried to conceal feelings of failure by adopting a facade of nonchalance, asserting that CSE 'was not worth it'. Many staff interpreted this response as 'confronting – a challenge to authority', and consequently Jim's initial feelings of positive anticipation in the fourth year were, in the fifth year, dampened by a realisation that he was not being entered for exams in any subject. No one had actually told him that from the outset he was a non-candidate for external examinations. There was almost a fatalist development towards that end, based upon self-fulfilling actions on the part of Jim and through the permanent labelling of his developmental status by staff.

Some staff held the invisible exam carrot above his head, hoping that the behavioural response from him would be conformity. In part it was, until he started to fail a series of hurdles, the highest being the mock examination. Every day during this two-week period Jim was expected to sit silently with his friends for three hours. Whilst his peers scribbled frantically to beat the clock, Jim just about wrote his name togehter with a few spasmodic lines and doodles. Understandably he became totally disillusioned and despondent, and started to question a curriculum which was not meeting his needs. This questioning found expression in disruptive behaviour.

Many of Jim's peers truanted during their fifth year, and silently they were allowed to do so. Jim, however, kept coming into school. Work experience seemed the answer. Jim was found placement with a local plumber and the experience afforded him feelings of success, away from the competitiveness of a situation in which he could not successfully compete. He was able to observe adults in a working role to which he was trying to aspire and he took his new-found status back into the school situation. The biggest spin-off for Jim was the prestige he felt because he was in a working situation. Enhanced feelings of self-worth were, however, short-lived. When he left school at Easter his work placement came to an end. He had failed in school and was now failing outside because he could not get work. Jim refused placement on a Youth Training Programme because, in his words, 'It is slave labour.'

In the present economic climate, youngsters who are less able regularly fail to obtain jobs in the competitive work market. It has been confirmed that in terms of unemployment more than twice as many of them faced some unemployment in comparison with their academically more able peers. It was also revealed that over a period of two years, ten times as many handicapped young people had been out of work for six months or more, than the non-handicapped who had left full-time education. Evidence is contained in a research project on the Employment of Handicapped School Leavers – Welher 1982, commissioned by the Warnock Committee (1975–7).

The situation has worsened significantly since that time. The Youth Training Scheme was supposedly a relevant and well-organised response to meet the growing crisis of mass youth unemployment. Interestingly, the Manpower Services Commission and the current government have consistently denied that this scheme is a response designed to occupy unemployed youngsters. They argue that in the absence of effective skill training in our schools a remediative response has to be offered in situations beyond school. Once trained, unemployable youngsters will then be able to obtain employment commensurate with their newly acquired skills. The reality for numerous youngsters is very different. Both the Inspectorate and the Further Education Unit express reservations about the scheme. Referring to a forthcoming HMI report, Melia emphasises that some YTS schemes are coping badly with those youngsters who would not normally have stayed on at school (Melia, *Times Higher Educational Supplement*, March 1987) while Mansell, the Further Education Unit's chief executive, saliently observes that 'the education system would never have got away with this type of record' (*Times Educational Supplement*, 6 March 1987).

The work placement for Jim was an expediency measure. Whilst many schools now have admirable programmes of work experience, how many, by sending youngsters on 'work' placements, are deluding them? The 'job' is seen at the centre of the placement instead of the experience with all its preparative and follow-up skill-based work within the school curriculum, which should essentially accompany that 'experience'. Expectations of a 'job' at the end of such placements are often unrealistically high. Many schools promulgate a curriculum which ironically fails the youngster in school, a consolidation of failure ensues – through unrealistic 'work' placement.

We are still struggling with redefinitions of the concept of work. In the interim it would perhaps be better to place youngsters on community projects, in voluntary as well as work-experience placements.

Within each of these case studies it is possible to discern some, if not all, of Erikson's distinct developmental demands. It is equally possible to isolate those pertinent achievement aspects which the youngsters are attempting to cope with. Staff development activities in the final chapter of this volume encourage staff to explore these case studies further.

The issue of whether needs are 'special' or 'general' is the subject of constant professional debate and controversy. The whole concept of needs is a value-laden one. What we do know in the classroom situation is that adolescents experience developmental difficulties which can regularly be translated into learning difficulties, and which demand a viable whole-school response.

The implications for the teacher in the classroom are clear. We have to be aware of both the developmental needs of youngsters and the achievement potential which is within each individual. An effective caring curricula response is one which is conducive to the development of this potential. This volume develops that view of special education.

Part Two The developing concept of pastoral care: meeting adolescents' special educational needs

The development of pastoral care is traced through three developmental processes. A consideration is made of the organisational placement of pastoral care which influences its effectiveness in the curriculum and three key themes of pastoral care are considered as positive responses to special educational needs.

—2——

Pastoral care: meeting adolescents' special needs

The purpose of this chapter is to analyse through a description of three identifiable processes, the development of pastoral care as an effective response to special educational needs.

THE DEVELOPING CONCEPT OF PASTORAL CARE

The Warnock Report made reference to the need for a 'framework' in which young people could develop competency and consequently could use 'of right', the facilities available in school. During the past fifteen years or so a 'framework' has been developing which has often been generously resourced, particularly in terms of staffing and scaled posts. Paradoxically, for years we appear to have ignored the efficacy of this secondary structure, which has often assumed a peripheral curriculum status in schools. By definition it is a caring curriculum influence which could shape an effective response to needs. Somehow in key debates about special education in secondary schools this resource has been ignored. Only scant reference is made to pastoral care in the chapter 'Transition to adult life' in the now almost standard reference text by Hegarty and Pocklington (1981). Indeed, very few theorists of special education have analysed the kernel of pastoral care and seen its integral links with special educational provision in the secondary curriculum. There are notable exceptions (Galloway, 1981; 1982; 1985). It may well be that this underfunctioning of pastoral care as a response to special educational needs has existed because of the differing concepts which people have held of pastoral care-concepts which have been reshaped, refined and evaluated continually over the past fifteen or so years. Although it is difficult to chart any curriculum innovation through precise stages it is possible to identify three developmental processes of pastoral care which have influenced a number of school climates within which I have worked. These reveal a range of ideological positions which influence the organisation and process of pastoral care within secondary schools.

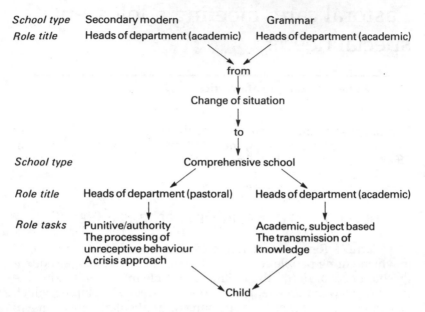

Situational influences – the emergence of the comprehensive school

School type   Secondary modern   Grammar
Role title   Heads of department (academic)   Heads of department (academic)

from

Change of situation

to

School type   Comprehensive school

Role title   Heads of department (pastoral)   Heads of department (academic)

Role tasks   Punitive/authority   Academic, subject based
                      The processing of   The transmission of
                      unreceptive behaviour   knowledge
                      A crisis approach

Child

Figure 2.1   *Pastoral care: process 1*

PROCESS ONE

With the growth of comprehensive education and the fusion of secondary-modern and grammar schools in the late 1960s and early 1970s there was a simultaneous need to amalgamate senior posts. In consequence this meant that many academic middle-management posts were retained by grammar-school personnel. Some secondary-modern school heads of department on the other hand found themselves in the position of being offered very different management roles within developing pastoral structures. It was not only because of the need to cater for the displaced middle-management secondary-modern staff that these posts were created. With increases in school size, youngsters were reorganised into manageable 'pastoral groups', in years or houses. Consequently, one key task of the heads of pastoral units was to 'manage' youngsters, particularly those who were actually or potentially disruptive. It was a crisis response, designed to maintain the system.

The developing concept of pastoral care in the amalgamated school has often been shaped by an authoritative, punitive view of 'care'. The academic departments were there to teach subjects. If a youngster misbehaved, then the problem was seen to be the youngster and not the teaching situation from which the problem emanated. Consequently the youngster was sent to the head of house or head of year for 'correction' and then returned 'processed' to the subject teacher.

Process one–an example of practice

Heads of pastoral units were in a dilemma and were faced with questions of accountability, particularly in relation to children with behavioural difficulties. Such heads were often the bridge between pupils and the teaching staff. The latter saw their role as teaching their subject and not teaching children with learning difficulties. Often this 'bridging' role was crisis-centred, dealing with the 'now' instead of long-term preventative or developmental responses.

Academic staff believed that one requirement of the head of pastoral unit was to uphold the status quo, supporting staff in whatever situation, and for whatever reason.

'If you send a lad to Mr ... 's room, all he does is give them a cup of tea and send them back and you know he's sided with them'.
'They all quieten down when Mrs ... arrives she doesn't take sides, and they know it. *You* always know she'll back you, and they know it'.

Heads of pastoral units, often for expediency, would remove a youngster from a fraught situation, attempt to counsel the child, but do little to alter the situation which had led up to and precipitated the problem behaviour. This punitive aspect of the role had evolved, not only because of perceptions of other staff, but also because many heads of pastoral units reluctantly accepted this negative disciplinary stance. It gave them instant credibility. They were seen to be 'doing something about pupils who are openly disruptive'. One senior member of the pastoral team regularly had pupils with behavioural difficulties lining up outside his room for the whole of the teaching day. The office was placed in a key focal position in the main entrance of the school. Consequently at break times their peers would walk past the detained pupils. This contributed to the anti-school picture which they held of themselves. Comments such as 'see yer later' (laughter), 'Who's been a bad boy?', swelled self-esteem, and enhanced the anti-authority stance which the school pastoral system inadvertently nurtured.

When asked how this approach helped such pupils, the reply was: 'Well at least it shows staff that I'm doing something and that I'm prepared to take responsibility for the kids'. This view was erroneous and naïve for several reasons:

(a) it absolved both teaching and tutoring staff of responsibility for pupils with behavioural difficulties in their group;
(b) it was but a temporary measure in that the situation from which the behaviour originated was untouched;
(c) the pupil identified with the anti-authority/school group and found supportive strength in this group; and
(d) the punitive relationship between the head of pastoral unit and the pupil negated any opportunity for positive pastoral work.

These negative perceptions of the role of head of pastoral unit filtered through to a wider group of pupils. One fairly new head of house recounted her experience when she decided to 'screen' small groups of second-year pupils in an attempt to pick up signs of disaffiliation from school and accompanying learning difficulties.

> 'One group of pupils stood outside my door, most apparently were the 'conforming, hard conscientious worker types' who had never seen the inside of the house office. The following anxious comments were heard:
> 'What do you think we've done?'
> 'I've never been sent to Miss ... before; my mum will kill me.'
> 'Do you think she's going to keep us in?'
> I heard shouts from children passing the end of the corridor:
> 'What's she got yer for?'
> 'Who's been naughty then?'
> The first screening session was spent trying to break down misunderstandings in an attempt to communicate to these pupils the positive pastoral focus of the role!'

Another head of pastoral unit commented:

> 'The kids who are always in trouble brag about being sent to the office. It's something to boast to their mates about, it does nothing in the long run. They keep coming back. I don't know what staff expect me to do, probably make them disappear. Some do, because if they're absent I don't chase them up, in fact I let some know that it's best if they don't come in, let them cool off for a bit.'

One head of department when asked about the role of the head of the pastoral unit commented: 'I wouldn't do it. The only thing I see is D. R. charging around school with bundles of papers in his hand, looking busy, chasing his tail, stopping to have a quick shout at someone outside his office ... yet again.'

The assertion that the teaching profession might regard guidance as 'a consciously evolved device for managing a potentially explosive situation' (Best *et al.* 1980) probably holds true when analysing many of the aspects of this concept of pastoral care. It shaped the 'emotional climate' of the school by:

- producing immediate gratification, particularly in that it convinced staff that something positive has been 'done to the pupils';
- instilling fear amongst younger pupils when they were sent to the pastoral office;
- producing an aura of cynicism and festering rebelliousness amongst many older pupils when 'sent' to the pastoral head;
- encouraging an increasingly violent atmosphere and potentially explosive situation;
- encouraging the tendency for staff to label possibly disturbed youngsters as just 'troublemakers';
- encouraging 'problem' staff to project the problems on to youngsters, instead of encouraging staff to analyse their responses, which may be inadequate.

In total such a system encouraged an overuse and misuse of a pastoral framework which had, as a prime aim, the containment of a wide range of youngsters, in order to maintain the equilibrium of the school organisation.

Figure 2.2   *Pastoral care: process 2*

Situational influences–the growth of counselling

Title	The school counsellor	Counsellor/head of pastoral unit
Role tasks	Understanding (contained within the counselling contract)	First aid, palliative approach (contained within the pastoral unit)

PROCESS TWO

Pastoral care in the 1970s had become firmly established as a permanent organisational structure. Deputy heads were now given overall responsibility for pastoral care, with middle-management personnel receiving enhanced scaled posts. Its response still focused, however, upon crisis situations, and pastoral care still adhered to a maintenance role. In addition to discipline, other administrative tasks were becoming incorporated within the role. For example:

- collating internal academic reports
- liaising with parents and outside agencies
- writing leaver's references

- administering behaviour reports
- writing court reports
- arranging work experience
- running general studies programmes for the less able and disaffected. (It seemed to follow that if one were in an official disciplinary role, then one also could actually teach the recalcitrant, hence one invariably had responsibility for General Studies and Lifeskills programmes)
- checking registers, liaising with EWOs
- checking uniform.

One head of house made a list of at least forty interrelated administrative duties, which at one time had been part of the workload of senior management and had now been delegated to middle-management pastoral roles!

On the positive side there were signs that the 'care' aspect of the role was becoming more defined and given greater prominence. The process of counselling started to underpin many 'pastoral' responses. This was accompanied by a growth of counsellor training courses in many universities and polytechnics. Whilst these courses initially focused upon counselling skills, there was a growing shift in emphasis within some courses which placed the lay skills of counselling at the centre of the pastoral and, increasingly, the teaching response.

Simultaneously, whilst the role of the school counsellor was becoming consolidated in some schools, many official middle-management pastoral roles were being reshaped and redefined because of the influence of the counselling movement. The counselling response came out of the counsellor's office and these skills of counselling were now being used by a growing number of pastoral heads within the school situation.

There was, however, a tendency for some of these pastoral heads to assume the therapeutic stance, to the exclusion of their educational role. Instead they became involved in a pseudo-therapeutic response to needs which confused many colleagues and youngsters.

One of the strengths of any pastoral system is to know when to refer a child for outside help. I have observed some children who have been retained within a school's pastoral framework on the assumption that the counsellor-trained pastoral head will somehow be able to meet the needs of the child. This assumes a first-aid, patching-up approach to pastoral care. The helping contract could be almost collusive. The youngster has the problems. He goes to the pastoral head to be counselled and then he is returned to the classroom situation. In a crisis there are those youngsters who need the opportunity just to talk and release tension. There are others who need something more than a bland 'understanding' response. Galloway raises the important question, 'What are the implications of a pastoral system which works from the premise that "to understand" is to forgive all?' (Galloway 1981). Such a view

(a) refocuses attention away from an often inadequate learning environment;
(b) does not encourage a youngster to look at himself realistically or to identify and 'own' the problem which he can then positively work upon to alleviate (additionally there are some youngsters who manipulate such a 'holding' situation);
(c) allows many staff to see the youngster being mysteriously and 'confidentially' helped by the pastoral head, but, in the absence of any constructive feedback, they retain a 'client' view of the pupil. The child is the one with the problems and is given the 'sickness' label.

Process two–an example of practice

The counsellor

Although paid a Scale 3 for academic responsibilities, the heads of subject departments were sometimes also asked to become pastoral heads. Staff were given this additional responsibility primarily because it would enhance their career prospects, and secondly because they were considered to be good disciplinarians and administrators. In theory the combination of the two roles could have facilitated movement towards a whole-school approach involving a close co-ordination of both pastoral and academic initiatives. Instead, a school counsellor (Scale 4) was appointed whose role was effectively to promulgate and enhance the 'care' aspect of pastoral care.

The school was organised on two neighbouring sites. One was the boys', the other the girls' school. The staff rooms were still run on rigid, sexist lines. The men congregated in the former male staff room, complete with appropriate 'male' magazines and sports trophies. The women's staff room was neater, cleaner, with chair back covers and an absence of cigarette smoke. All the heads of year were males. Consequently the pastoral process operated from the male base.

The female counsellor deliberately had her office situated in this building, on the understanding that she could liaise more effectively with the heads of year. She was observed, over a year, using very high-level counselling skills: empathy, understanding, listening, moving the client forward and problem-solving with a number of very disturbed and distraught youngsters. There were many self-referrals. There were also youngsters referred by heads of year. However this form of organisation negated the whole-school approach for a number of reasons:

(a)   Many staff felt suspicious of a comparatively well-paid member of staff who listened to students' problems but gave very little feedback. The view was that there was often collusion between the counsellor and the client.

(b)   Some heads of year felt understandably that they were helping the student by referring, but such a response did little to change their regularly rigid attitudes to youngsters.

(c)   Some youngsters permanently held on to the fact that they had a counsellor, and they were never weaned off this process.

(d)   The educative process within the classroom remained untouched, the class teaching situation was not seen as having a specific contribution to the therapeutic process.

The head of house

He had been trained as a marriage guidance counsellor. He had also just completed a part-time certificate course in counselling. He therefore believed that the main thrust of this role was to help youngsters with problems in a crisis situation and that meant counselling them individually. Within the upper school curriculum many youngsters were totally uncatered for due to the academic emphasis of the teaching. They therefore used the pastoral head as a safety valve for some of their frustrations. They were additionally able to remove themselves physically from some potentially explosive classroom situations. If youngsters were sent out of lessons, the head of house accepted them at the house office, probed for and listened to their grievances. A record player played continuously in the house common room. Within this room many of his 'problem brood' would congregate, sitting in a bored, lethargic manner, but at least they were removed from a potentially harmful confrontation situation. Some would come from lessons with the taut request/ultimatum: 'I'm not going back to his ... lesson, or coming to this ... school again.'

The response to some youngsters from the head of year was to find them work experience. Others, if they truanted, were not too rigorously followed up. There were, however, instances where the pastoral head, in his helping role, almost felt he had a mission to counsel. One fifth-year boy felt so pressurised through being continually asked to 'Tell me your problems. I understand, I've been through it', that he went to a senior member of staff requesting that she get the head of house 'off my back'.

Within this process many pastoral staff were largely ineffective because they held vague ideas as to how pastoral care ought to be implemented. It was often seen as merely offering 'emotional first aid' (Hamblin, 1978). Teachers saw pastoral care solely in terms of 'getting to know' children, and in becoming involved in individual crisis relationships with pupils. They falsely believed that 'to understand is to forgive'. This removed any real incentive for the teacher to look at the underlying processes which may be exacerbating the child's problems.

Spooner's comment could also apply to this exclusively forgiving and understanding approach: 'You do not when children find food difficult to digest, excuse them from eating', (Galloway, 1981). Instead an efficient tutor questions and actively restructures the curriculum which is being presented whilst simultaneously assisting the child to develop the skills necessary to negotiate that curriculum.

Figure 2.3 *Pastoral care: process 3*

Situational influences: 'The whole-school/child approach'

- the theorisation of pastoral care and its professional establishment within the mainstream curriculum
- links between pastoral and teaching approaches
- skills-based teaching/the development of a distinct personal and social education programme
- the development of the process approach in core curriculum initiatives

PROCESS THREE

The 1980s have brought about a growing critical analysis of pastoral care. One assertion is that statements about pastoral care are inclined to be 'woolly prescriptions for what it ought to be rather than realistic assessments of what actually goes on in schools' (Best *et al.*, 1980). This comment clearly articulates the view held by many educationalists that pastoral care is in danger of becoming an ambivalent and loose concept practised by people who have very different perceptions of its functions, and in particular the needs of pupils which it purports to meet.

Hamblin asserted that 'Pastoral care is not something set apart from the daily work of the teacher. It is that element of the teaching process which centres around the personality of the pupil and the forces in his environment' (Hamblin, 1978).

Pastoral care involves direct intervention in the teaching and learning programme. It has to merge with the whole educative thrust of the school.

Process three–an example of practice

The underlying tenet of this pastoral process was that the special needs, pastoral care and academic strands of the secondary-school curriculum linked with and impinged upon each other. Such a view had implications for the school management structure.

Management changes

Previously there had been a deputy head (curriculum), deputy head (pastoral) and a deputy head (timetable). The pastoral curriculum of the school officially was the responsibility of heads of year under the direction of heads of lower and upper schools. The academic curriculum was the responsibility of subject heads under the direction of faculty heads. Influenced by the concept of an integrated curriculum, the senior management structure was redefined and restructured.

The underlying philosophy behind this change of title and role designation was that the curriculum incorporated the academic, special and pastoral-care aspects of the school. The unity of the curriculum would depend upon the co-ordinating effectiveness ascribed to the management roles of the head, deputies and senior teachers. One of the aims of the redefined management structure was to allow for a greater curriculum cohesiveness, enabling staff to become involved actively in cross-curriculum development.

The particular school was a rural comprehensive and was pastorally organised into lower and upper schools. In addition to adopting a redesigned management and curriculum structure it became a TVEI pilot school, and it consequently had to grapple with many of the demands placed upon it through the introduction of this curriculum initiative. Its TVEI scheme attracted the attention of a number of positive evaluative studies. The whole-school guidance programme, with its stress upon active tutorial sessions, elicited commendable comments from HMI. The school's curriculum links with the community, which developed from strands in the pastoral-care programme, was recognised as a positive curriculum innovation by the Society of Education Officers, resulting in the school achieving a Curriculum Award for this area of development.

No schemes of this kind are without their problems. This was no exception. There were many staff who felt shell-shocked by the implications which the innovation could have for them in the

1 Curriculum responsibility — governors/headteacher
2 Curriculum direction – deputy heads
  (curriculum development, timetable, professional staff development)
3 Curriculum co-ordination – senior teachers (heads of curriculum development – lower/upper schools)
  (promotion of unity of academic and pastoral aims, no separate senior teacher academic or pastoral)
4 Curriculum implementation – all staff

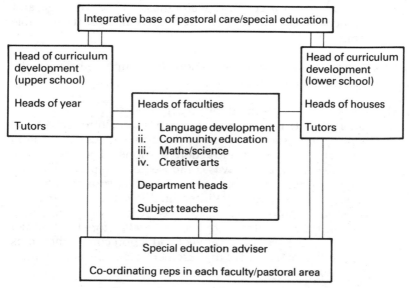

Figure 2.4 *Integrated curriculum–a management structure*

classroom. Although such change caused anxiety, it also created awareness, and staff started to question, develop and refine their own teaching roles. Because of the generous funding which backed the TVEI initiative, the scheme produced equally generous resourcing for some curriculum areas.

In addition to the help given to youngsters with special needs, both on a withdrawal and within-class basis, all youngsters experienced the guidance programme which complemented special-needs provision both in the lower and upper schools.

PRIMARY AIMS OF UPPER-SCHOOL GUIDANCE PROGRAMME

The following primary aims underpinned the upper-school guidance programme, which was seen as an integral part of the school's TVEI initiative and special educational emphasis:

(a)   to enable the school to meet some of the diverse developmental needs of adolescents;
(b)   to help the student to develop and find constructive solutions to his problems of self-awareness and social adjustment;
(c)   to encourage students to acquire skills, experience and knowledge of the changing concept of work, and to encourage resources and a willingness to accept change; and
(d)   to encourage the development of skills which are transferable from school to work.

These general aims were operationally defined through the following programme components:

(1)   *Induction courses* (4th/5th/6th year)
Upon entry to the upper school, pupils were introduced to the expectations and traditions of the upper-school curriculum through a series of induction sessions. The sixth form induction programme was composed of two parts. The first was a 'general' induction course of approximately two sessions to enable any 'intending' sixth-former to make constructive informed decisions before he became an 'actual' intending 'committed sixth-former', well before the summer term. A more specific one-week induction course then took place either at the end of the summer term or the beginning of the autumn term.

(2)   *Study skills*
Included such issues as: what are study skills?; personal study habits; the study environment; concentration; reading for learning; note-taking; essay techniques; coping with stress; group support; examination anxiety; studying for examinations; examination techniques; and self-assessment.

(3)   *Personal and social development*
The emphasis was upon encouraging pupils to develop an adequate self-concept based upon how they view and assess themselves and how, in their relations with other people, they are viewed by those people. There was also an element of health education in this component. This reflective enquiry was based upon experiential learning derived from work and community experience placements.

(4)   *Pre-vocational community involvement*
Experiential learning, coping with unemployment, work search skills, presentation of self.

(5)   *Self-assessment*

Self-assessment permeated the four components. Pupils were encouraged to assess internal school reports and, with the help of form staff, look at ways of acting upon guidance given in these reports. Assessment was also based upon employers' reports from work experience. It was in essence a formative as opposed to a summative procedure.

All these components were interrelated. There are frequently no distinct divisions between educational, vocational and personal problems and their resolutions. All contribute towards the development of the young person and affect how he tackles achievement aspects specified earlier. Translating the theory into workable practice entailed changes in roles, tasks and procedures. There was an enormous amount of commitment amongst staff. Official curriculum development meetings increased and, contrary to the popular view of the length of a teacher's day, meetings regularly extended hours after school had officially closed. The placement and timing of these meetings were, however, totally inadequate. Management and curriculum-development meetings cannot just be tagged on to the end of a school day. They have to be a top priority in developing the curriculum process, and as such should be built into the official school day. This issue will be explored in the final chapter of this volume.

A placement dilemma: pastoral care and special needs–periphery or core?

The purpose of this chapter is to consider the organisational placement and influence of pastoral care as a response to special educational needs within the curriculum.

PERIPHERAL CURRICULUM INITIATIVES

A whole-school approach to special educational needs demands a careful analysis of how the curriculum is organised and managed. Sayer (1987) expounds upon this process, 'A curricular organisation capable of identifying individual and group needs is unlikely to be so fragmented as much secondary school practice has been in the past.'

There have been a wide range of innovative curriculum components on offer for a very long time in secondary schools. These have shaped and positively influenced the curriculum climate for numerous young people. They have, however, often functioned in a fragmented and compartmentalised way, on the sidelines of the mainstream curricula. Two distinct examples have been special education and pastoral care.

Because such initiatives have often been a compensatory response to young people who would not otherwise have been catered for in the mainstream, they have been accorded a low status within the traditional curriculum, even though their contribution to the developmental needs of youngsters, particularly those labelled less able and/or disaffected, has regularly been of considerable benefit.

Functioning on the periphery, such activities have found themselves in what is analagous to 'spectator' roles in relation to the dominant purpose of school. The iniatives have supported the youngsters involved in them but they have not unduly affected what has gone on in the mainstream curriculum. Indeed many such initiatives have been a safety valve (a special school within the main school?) for some curriculum structures which have woefully failed a high proportion of youngsters.

Yet in spite of such pressures, these peripheral curricula initiatives regularly show evidence of high positive learning environments. Youngsters and staff have been observed by the writer to show enormous loyalty and affection for each other within an atmosphere of trust and care. A comment regularly expressed by people who work in these curriculum areas is that 'It's a bit like being in a primary school.' The processes of a number of these peripheral curriculum areas may well reflect primary-school practices and values which encourage active negotiation and problem-solving by students and staff.

Through such curriculum forms the young person, within a supportive group environment, is able to negotiate achievement demands by actively solving problems and taking responsibility for his own learning. Such processes are the base strand of positive self-growth and they enable youngsters to cope with those key issues of development expounded upon by Erikson (1968). Although enhanced feelings of self-worth may be experienced within these curriculum areas, full participation in the mainstream curriculum, however, is being denied some youngsters.

Youngsters developing with some peripheral curriculum forms experience group cohesiveness and are valued as individuals; this is vividly illustrated by Sue Johnson in Chapter 8. Many of the youngsters in the case study participated in work and community projects and they consolidated these experiences by being able to express feelings within the safe, non-threatening environment of the group. One has to ask: who is being denied access to a positive learning climate? If the sentiments of the Warnock Report regarding the aims of education hold true:

> They are, first, to enlarge a child's knowledge, experience and imaginative understanding, and thus his awareness of moral values and capacity for enjoyment; and secondly, to enable him to enter the world after formal education is over as an active participant in society and a responsible contributor to it, capable of achieving as much independence as possible.
>
> (Warnock Report, 1978, para. 1.4)

Should not these curriculum experiences be for all youngsters? There were numerous 'mainstream' youngsters in Sue Johnson's case-study school who were excluded from the experiences of the 'City and Guilds' group. They continually requested that they be included in the group. The demand was very apparent.

Whilst it is recognised that the process of pastoral care in numerous schools is being practically realised through a range of very positive pastoral programmes which in some instances do operate on the curriculum periphery, this volume stresses the potency of pastoral care as an all-pervasive curriculum influence. This is not to ignore the fact that there are some professionals who still argue for its retention as a separate curriculum component. One understandable reason is that they wish to establish the potency of pastoral care initially through distinct programmes. Wilensky offers a pertinent view of the development of professionalisation:

> Any occupation wishing to exercise professional authority must find a technical basis for it, assert an exclusive jurisdiction, link both skill and jurisdiction to standards of training, and convince the public that its services are uniquely trustworthy
>
> (Wilensky, 1964).

He observes a distinct three-stage process to professionalisation:

- start doing full-time the thing that needs doing
- establish a training school and
- combine to form a professional association.

The competent are separated from the less competent through the designation of distinct tasks to complementary role holders, and so a professional line-management structure is formed.

It is conjectured that this process is beginning to be reflected through the professionalisation of pastoral care. Initially there was an urgent need for pastoral carers to create professional awareness of pastoral care and consider the ends and means of the pastoral process. It is now an opportune time for the pastoral-care movement to analyse how it can shape and influence many of the current curriculum initiatives, and in so doing blur its own professional edges. Its credibility as a whole curriculum influence depends upon how ready it is to evaluate it own distinct professional identity within the context of the whole-school approach to needs.

What does this mean for the implementation of pastoral care in secondary schools now? It is at an interesting stage of development. There are some who argue that pastoral care, if it is truly an integrative component of the curriculum, should eventually burn itself out when it starts to underpin other current secondary initiatives. Distinct 'official' pastoral posts are an anomaly in a whole curriculum response to pastoral care and special needs.

A CORE PASTORAL CURRICULUM?

Three influential and related core developments are those promulgated by the Further Education Unit, the Joint Board for Pre-Vocational Education and the Manpower Services Commission, which all emphasise the process of learning and reflect the pastoral process. The FEU, influenced by the recommendations of HMI (1983), argue for a series of core entitlement aims which every youngster should follow.

Figure 3.1 *Core entitlement aims (FEU, April 1985)*

ADAPTABILITY
ROLE TRANSITION
PHYSICAL SKILLS
INTERPERSONAL SKILL
VALUES
COMMUNICATION/NUMERACY
PROBLEM-SOLVING
INFORMATION TECHNOLOGY
SOCIETY
LEARNING SKILLS
HEALTH EDUCATION
CREATIVITY
ENVIRONMENT
SCIENCE AND TECHNOLOGY
COPING

These aims are pervasive and as such they allow for a wide interpretation of curriculum organisation and delivery.

The core should not be regarded as a syllabus to be worked through from start to finish uniformly with all pupils, but a diagnostic and planning check list, from which individual programmes can be constructed. Such a check list should be regarded as dynamic and not static   (FEU, April 1985).

A succinct comment is that 'it (the core) should be as much a basis for counselling and guidance in life-skills as for choosing academic and/or vocational subjects' (FEU, April 1985). In other words the core aims should enable a curriculum to be succinctly relevant to the developmental needs of adolescents. Similar core aims characterise the Certificate for Pre-Vocational Studies (see Figure 3.2).

Again the four general aims of CPVE relate closely to Erikson's (1968) four issues of adolescent development and ILEA's (Hargreaves Report, 1984) four achievement aspects. They are additionally reflected in the Technical Vocational Educational Initiative encouraged by the MSC. It provides a bridge between the rigid boundaries of 14–16 and the 16–18 education programme and it has core similarities both to the Joint Board recommendations and to the FEU entitlement aims: 'There is an obvious connection between our proposals for such a core and the curriculum design encouraged by TVEI' (FEU/SCDC, 1985)

These core developments are generic and dynamic and stress the importance of the curriculum process which, according to the Joint Board, should include:

• activity based learning

Figure 3.2   *Certificate of Pre-Vocational Education (Joint Board for Pre-Vocational Education, 1985)*

Aims

(a)   assists the transition from school to adulthood by further equipping the young people with the basic skills, experiences, attitudes, knowledge and personal and social competences required for success in adult life including work
(b)   provides individually relevant educational experience which encourages learning and achievement
(c)   provides young people with recognition of their attainments through a qualification which embodies national standards
(d)   provides opportunities for progression to continuing education, training and/or work

Contents

The contents will include:

(i)   *a core area* of activities which will foster the development of skills, knowledge and attitudes
      personal and career development
      industrial, social and environmental studies
      communication
      social skills
      numeracy
      science and technology
      information technology
      creative development
      practical skills
      problem-solving
(ii)   *vocational studies* based upon a modular approach (i.e. 'a set of experiences and outcomes which may be achieved through a variety of appropriate learning methods')
(iii)   *additional studies* taking up a maximum of 25 per cent of the course time. Within this area students have the opportunity to develop personal interests. (This section is not compulsory, if youngsters wish to focus upon (i) and (ii) they have that choice.)

- experience and practically based learning
- well organised work experience
- underpinning by guidance and counselling
- negotiated forms of learning and
- recording of achievements through a process of systematic profiling.

(Joint Board for Pre-Vocational Education, 1985)

All are essentially caring pastoral processes which should respond effectively to the perceived needs of youngsters. Pastoral care within these core initiatives is not seen as a programme. It is a pervasive influence which can produce a total pastoral caring ethos in a whole-school response to special educational needs.

—4——————————————————————

The key themes of pastoral care: responses to special educational needs

The purpose of this chapter is to analyse three pastoral themes which can make an effective response to the special educational needs of adolescents.

It was illustrated in Chapter 1 that both the Hargreaves Report (1984) and Erikson (1968) provide useful guidelines for the teacher involved in assessing adolescent developmental needs. Figure 4.1 recounts these guidelines and indicates interrelated pastoral themes which can make a positive response to these needs.

Four achievement aspects (Hargreaves, 1984)	**Four dimensional issues** (Erikson, 1968)
● traditional learning	● personal and social development
● practical application of knowledge	● vocational development
● personal and social skills	● becoming sexually committed
● motivation, commitment and confidence	● acquiring values which will shape ideological commitments

The pastoral response
● personal and social education
● vocational and pre-vocational education
● study skills

Figure 4.1 *Pastoral care and development needs*

It is useful at this point to elaborate upon these interrelated themes before considering the actual processes of the pastoral curriculum.

KEY THEMES IN A CORE PASTORAL CURRICULUM

The interlinking themes of personal and social education, vocational/pre-vocational education and study skills can make an effective core-curriculum response to a range of achievement demands with which young people have to cope. Whilst the themes are educationally indivisible, there is value in considering them separately, because they can then be evaluated and their implications for whole-school curriculum development assessed.

Personal and social education

When considering the issue of group dynamics, Button stated 'To be human is to be in relationship with other people' (1981). Only a few disillusioned and injured people could reject this premise. If one does accept it, then one has to take it a step further and say that education is about being human and this involves interacting with other people. Such interactions have to be the essence of the educative experience. Personal and social development encourages the youngster to look at himself in relation to other people and to analyse the quality of this relationship. Before he can see himself as a positive and participatory group member he has to consider how he relates to and values himself as an individual. This is the underlying activity associated with Erikson's developmental stage five, which was introduced in Chapter 1 of this volume.

The curriculum, if it is to relate positively to developmental needs, has to make a response to resolve the adolescent's confusion. Decisions have to be made within a total curriculum which encourage young people to engage in a process of reflective enquiry, looking at the reasons for behaviour and to acquire the maturity and self-confidence to take responsibility for and accept the consequences of actions. Peter, for example, in the Chapter 8 case study, came to the group determined to create a tough impression. We focused upon this hard facade and eventually encouraged him to look at the reasons why he was acting in this manner. Initially some of the youngsters were anxious and afraid, but subsequently they started to ignore him. It was only when he admitted that he did not really like being 'a loner' that the group response started to touch him noticeably. He gradually realised that his behaviour affected how people reacted to him in the group.

The Schools Council Moral Education Project is organised to encourage the individual to look at the consequences of actions initially by analysing demands of the self in a group situation and of the costs and benefits to the individual and society of the alternative courses available.

Although it is now a little dated (having been published in 1972), the issues raised are still pertinent to the developmental needs of young people. The curriculum processes upon which the project was based now underpin many current secondary initiatives. It is provocatively fresh and inspirational as a curriculum resource, particularly within personal and social education, 'The material provides no "right" answers, but the general rule of consider the needs, feelings and interests of those involved permeates the project' (McPhail, 1972).

Such material encourages us not only to assess our methods of teaching, but it also asks us to be prepared to analyse ourselves and our actions, as well as those of youngsters within the teaching situation.

In personal and social education, the content, which is the subject of current debate, is not so important as considerations about the processes which underly this curriculum component. The pertinent issue is about the cyclical development of self within a social situation: the ways in which the self influences and is influenced by the environment. This has to be the thrust of any personal and social development programme. It represents a process through which both the general needs and the special needs of the adolescents can be recognised and worked through.

Vocational and pre-vocational education

Vocational education is a reflection of those curriculum aims, objectives and processes which underpin personal and social education and which are discernible in a number of current core secondary initiatives referred to in the previous chapter. Vocational education has to be an enabling curriculum which allows a youngster to cope with those developmental demands described in Figure 4.1.

Observation in the school situation reveals that whilst many aims and objectives may be rhetorically commendable they are not necessarily reflected within the curriculum process. Brennan's study illustrated that in only two out of every five secondary schools observed was there evidence of success in courses for school leavers (Brennan, 1979).

Brennan's questionnaire revealed that numerous school leavers with special educational needs underfunctioned in situations after leaving school because they did not have enhanced skills of social interaction. One salient reason for this skill retardation was the inadequacy of pastoral curriculum content and processes:

- counselling and guidance did not support and consolidate some of the skills being taught; many teachers thought that the employers could do the explaining
- many pupils were unable to transfer skills learnt in the school situation to the work situation
- preparation and follow-up involvement in work experience was poor
- discipline boundaries–the behaviour expected of pupils–was ill defined and
- very few schools followed up the post-school careers of the pupils.

(Brennan, 1979)

Vocational experience within the community

The aim of community education is to provide an educative experience which encourages students to develop as individuals, as well as distinct group members, within a flexible and supportive learning environment. This flexible learning environment places demands upon the school as an institution. It has to be prepared to influence and be influenced by the wider community via the process of a blurring of institutional boundaries.

Work experience

Work experience for pupils in their last year of compulsory education became permissible under the terms of the Education (Work Experience) Act 1973. According to the Act, the aim of work experience is to give pupils 'planned experience of a restricted range of types of employment as part of an education programme ... whilst experiencing the attitudes and relationships which are found in a work situation'. Experiential learning in the community, of which work experience is a part, facilitates a transfer of learning skills from the school situation to a wider societal sphere. Any learning can only be meaningful and internalised if it is based upon active participatory learning situations, situations which present opportunities for youngsters to observe and participate in different social relationships.

Laslett observes that self-criticism, friendliness, ability to get on with others, sensitivity to the feelings of others are 'a measure of a child's success' (Laslett, 1977). Through work experience placement, opportunities for success can be created in the wider community.

A work-experience placement

Jason was a lethargic and potentially disruptive student. He had a very low level of self-esteem and interpreted any criticism as a personal attack. He had associated numeracy and literacy difficulties. The pacing of learning in many of his lessons was too fast for him. Understandably he became totally uninterested in his studies. He had been found placement in a garage for his work experience. The old man who ran the forecourt oversaw the work which Jason undertook. Both individuals had difficulty in relating positively to each other. Some of the symptoms and reasons for this situation are illuminated in Brennan's questionnaire findings:

Jason

   (i) could not cope with leg pulling;
  (ii) interpreted a number of constructive criticisms as personal ridicule;
 (iii) was very inadequate in his initial dealings with customers;
 (iv) could not mentally work out the money transactions; and
  (v) was a poor timekeeper.

On the other hand the old man was

   (i) highly critical of, in his view, the failure of comprehensives to teach the '3Rs';
  (ii) expected Jason to be conversant with all the garage procedures after the first day;
 (iii) did not fully explain to Jason the basic procedures which needed adhering to;
 (iv) made 'generation' jokes which the youngster could not shrug off; and
  (v) did not explain to Jason the necessity of good timekeeping; instead he rang up the school to complain about Jason's behaviour.

Within the safety of the tutor-group situation a number of these issues were raised with Jason, for example, 'Initial dealings with customers'. In a rôle-play/simulation situation he was able to see a range of communication patterns acted out. Personal issues were raised which he was not aware of and consequently the session enabled these to be explored further. The aim was to develop

Jason's skills of social interaction. Before he could do this, however, awareness had to be created in him that there was a possible need for change.

The exploration of Jason's behaviour was not divorced from considerations about the behaviour of the old man. Participation in role play and simulation exercises allowed Jason and the whole group to explore sensitively a wide range of behaviour displayed by the employer. This encouraged the group to explore the idea that social behaviour is not an isolated activity, that it involves responsible social interaction.

Vocational education and work experience – the changing concept of work

There is a view expressed that in a time of growing unemployment it is unrealistic to place youngsters in work-experience situations. The letter illustrated in Figure 4.2 is written by a grandparent of a youngster who was placed in work experience.

The writer's concept of work was that if you did any work for anyone, then you received payment in return. We have to redefine and re-analyse the concept of work. Work must include a consideration of alternatives to paid employment. Instead of encouraging work-experience placements, we have to examine the wider arena of community-based placements including voluntary work. Within these situations young people will be able to liaise realistically with adults who are engaged in work activities which are not traditionally paid work whilst still experiencing an involvement in the wider community. This idea is already meeting with considerable opposition from certain pressure groups. That does not invalidate its worth to students.

The curriculum has always promulgated the work ethic. The promise has been that in return for hard academic school work and good behaviour there will be a job at the end of schooling. That has now changed. Interestingly, whereas in the past we could label the 'less able' as 'disruptive' because they would not, indeed regularly could not, conform to the demands of the academic strait-jacket, more academically able youngsters now express concerns and question the validity of an emphasis upon the traditional academic curriculum. They now see that the end result of this process does not necessarily produce a job. Unemployment as an issue is currently highly contentious, but if we are in the business of preparing young people for life after school, then schools have to address it.

For pupils with learning difficulties the issue is of greater significance than for others. Numerous manual jobs are now being replaced by automated techniques and whilst the Youth Training

PART B

For your information your son will be
undertaking Work Experience with the following
organisation:-

Person(s) or body	Type of work to be undertaken	Length of work experience
	Nurseryman	Every Wednesday, Thursday and Friday from week beginning

I am not Satidfide with the work he is has be docing not eueing giung him Pocket money so he has just as well be at. scholle when I was 12 years old I got 2/6 aweek. so you will say the times have changed but give me back the old Days. We did not work for nothing to fill orther Poples pockets. I am his Ground forther If you uold like to speake to me you are wellcome. thanking yous Yours his Grandfarther

Figure 4.2.

Scheme may temporarily serve as a panacea for the disenchant-
ment of most of our students with learning difficulties, there is in
reality faint optimism regarding many of their employment
opportunities.

The issue of unemployment – responses from young people and parents

A group of youngsters with special educational needs, who
experienced most of their curriculum in a special-needs department, were asked whether they thought that the school should
teach them about unemployment. Their parents were also asked

for their views. The comments illuminate a variety of anxieties, needs and concerns.

Young people

Of course you should teach us about unemployment ... it's there isn't it?

It's alright for you, you've got a job.

You'd be selling us short if you didn't.

Mr Thomas told us the other day, you learn your maths and you'll get a job ... then he told us off for laughing.

I want to know what to do the day after I leave this place and I haven't got a job.

What's so bad about not having a job?

If we don't have jobs then we've got spare time ... tell us about things to do in our spare time it you can't tell us about jobs.

We saw a film showing YTS kids working in a chicken factory ... you tell me, who's going to work in a chicken joint, just so that they can say they've got a job?

Getting a job is about getting money, you can get money other ways, you tell us some!

I've no idea about filling in dole forms.

If there aren't jobs, why can't I set up my own business, then I could employ all me mates.

Parents

It's not for a school to encourage kids to be unemployed ... you should be encouraging them to go out and find work.

There's work to be done ... it's no good teaching them that there isn't.

They hear enough about unemployment on the telly. They don't want to start hearing about it at school as well!

He's taking his exams so that he can get a job, why tell him that he can't?

We should be telling them about real life ... and real life is that there is no work.

I wish I'd been taught about things like claiming dole, even now I know there's things I must be entitled to, but nobody tells you how.

What's the use of science and art to you ... when you know that they won't look at you for street cleaning unless you've got a higher degree!

It doesn't seem right somehow, that schools should be teaching about unemployment. It almost seems as though you are telling them to give up ... instead of fighting for a right to work.

It would be interesting to see what the teacher response would be. What is salutary is that these comments keenly illustrate that young people are now demanding that this issue be tackled within the school situation. It is a more pressing issue for those students who may have difficulties with numeracy, literacy or oracy, and who cannot cope with the traditional demands contained in Achievement aspect one. In the realistic knowledge that unemployment is round the corner, they ask for a helping response from the school.

The views of parents were however, somewhat less unanimous. They had been through a system which had prepared them for a job. To say that the system should now be preparing youngsters to cope with unemployment was tantamount to adopting a fatalistic view of unemployment. 'Education should be fighting against it. It's no good schools putting other ideas into their heads.'

This same sentiment would be echoed by the current government, and possibly quite a few teachers. The point which has been missed however is that unemployment, particularly long-term unemployment, exists. For a large number of those youngsters designated as having special educational needs it is increasingly becoming the end product of schooling. The school can either pretend that unemployment does not exist or make both a viable moral and educational response to meet developing needs.

It has been observed that very few schools have actually tackled the issue of unemployment within their careers programmes for a number of reasons:

(1) teachers feel that they do not have first-hand experience of unemployment or the competence to teach the issue effectively;
(2) they are aware that it is a highly political and emotional issue;
(3) there is a fear that by raising the issue, students may start questioning not only the work ethic of wider society but that promulgated within the school situation; and
(4) there is a hostile reaction to teaching about unemployment because it could have a distinct labelling and conditioning effect on specific groups of youngsters who are already disaffected from school.

(Watts, 1978)

Some of the reasons given for not examining the issue of unemployment could apply to a number of controversial societal issues which remain untouched within the curriculum. If schools are preparing young people for life after school, then this issue cannot be ignored. The crux is the quality of that response. This is affected by the willingness of the staff to look at what they are offering within a vocational programme, and then to analyse whether it is equipping youngsters to negotiate life immediately after school.

With the expansion of YTS and school/college-based linked training initiatives, schools may well find themselves having to respond to transitional issues related to school and alternative forms of training, rather than about unemployment. In reality, however, this often means that the issue of unemployment will be removed from the school situation to further education. The curriculum need however is there, both within the school or FE institution.

Changes in working patterns between further education and schools

Tertiary education

A tertiary college is formed by the amalgamation within a geographical area of school sixth forms and a further education college. There are two important aspects to this form of organisation:

- it bridges the traditions of the academic and vocational curriculum and
- it allows a continuum of educational provision for students with a wide range of special educational needs.

This bridge across traditional learning boundaries develops the comprehensive principle within further education. The continuity of curriculum experience for 14–19 year olds ensures that extensive and close links are developed between feeder comprehensive schools and the college. For example, one college special-needs co-ordinator contacted neighbouring comprehensive schools, inviting youngsters who had special educational needs to participate in a 'taster' course during their last year of schooling. A group of youngsters at feeder comprehensive schools who had quite severe learning difficulties attended the college on one day per week. This experience gradually introduced them to the college atmosphere before most of them embarked on a formal 'bridge' course at the college after leaving school. The work undertaken on the 'taster' course developed work being followed in the vocational preparation programme in the school. More importantly, both the FE and the school member of staff undertook teaching responsibility in each other's institutions which gave confidence to the youngsters and facilitated a consistent continuum of provision between institutions.

The mainstream curriculum of both schools and FE are developing innovatory links, particularly through the framework of the Technical and Vocational Educational Initiative (TVEI). In the collaborative document produced by FEU/SCDC, the comment is made, 'Inevitably TVEI cuts across much that has been the traditional preserve of both schools and FE' (FEU/SCDC, 1985).

A comprehensive curriculum based upon a concept of a continuum of needs is a necessary educational response for those youngsters who at 16-plus experience a paucity of educational opportunities.

Given the pace and direction of change in 14–19 curriculum patterns, there is a distinct and urgent need for advocates of special educational provision, both within school and FE, to become active contributors to 14–19 curriculum design and development. Whilst the rhetoric of intentions is highly worth while, practical implementation is harder to achieve. There are localised pockets of exciting innovation which are consistently well-documented. Tertiary education is gradually being introduced in a number of LEAs. Within numerous FE colleges there is advocacy for the introduction of a matrix system of organisation as opposed to strict departmental divisions. In the light of these developments we have to encourage a whole-college approach to special educational provision.

We have units for youngsters with special needs in FE which reveal positive caring approaches to youngsters. However, the question remains: does such an organisation and management substantially change the awareness levels of lecturing staff across the whole college?

Further education still adheres to a prevailing concept of special education which, through its sympathetic and consequently patronising focus, places youngsters into categories of handicap, i.e. the blind, the deaf, the physically impaired, the YTS group, the severely subnormal.

One college lecturer was participating in an LEA special-needs training session run for workshop staff. He recalled one 'special-needs girl' who had opted for a six-hour block in the basic fundamentals of wallpapering. When she arrived at the session the lecturer discovered that she could already wallpaper. What, therefore, was he to do with her? When it was suggested that he could have encouraged her to use wallpapering techniques to cover shapes, waste-paper bins, pencil cases, or perhaps make rough designs for wallpaper patterns, he exclaimed that that was art. He was a wallpaperer, and she was also 'special needs'! We have to unlock the compartmentalised view of special education. Within further education colleges this holds implications for management and curriculum organisation.

In addition to advocating regional co-ordination, Warnock emphasised the need for a college co-ordinator who would be 'responsible for the welfare of students with special needs in the college and for briefing other members of staff on their special needs' (Warnock Report, 1978, Ch. 10, section 42). It is essential that this advocacy role for staff involved in meeting special educational needs extends the concept of special education both within and outside FE. Whilst it is accepted that it is remediative in so much as it responds to current distinct needs of youngsters in the college, more urgently it has to assume a key management and curriculum development role which is both preventative and pre-emptive in nature.

This entails (i) raising staff, student and parental awareness levels of special education within the college; and (ii) liaising with secondary schools and other organisations which are actively involved in the development of innovative organisational forms which can collectively deliver effective 14–19 provision.

The advocates of special education have to become active participants in 14–19 curriculum developments. To remain static is to subscribe to a view of special education which sees its heroic mission as being solely remediative and first-aid in nature. Such a stance has little effect upon current mainstream initiatives which are now, ironically, promulgating within their core many of the processes of education commonly thought to be 'special'–processes which are focused upon in the following part of this volume.

Study skills

Attitudes are shaped by experiences, and if young people continually experience feelings of failure, then it follows that they will adopt negative attitudes within the school situation. One view is that a school 'which does not set out to provide guidance for achievement as an integral part of pastoral care is likely not only to have underfunctioning pupils, but to be an underfunctioning school' (Hamblin, 1981).

There are some curriculum forms which inculcate youngsters into believing that they cannot achieve. Instead they become passive recipients of packages of knowledge which they cannot use in an applied situation. Other curriculum forms however encourage youngsters actively to negotiate and participate in the learning environment. Ironically, even in some of those curricula which encourage active learning, the youngster still cannot actively negotiate, because he has not the skills to participate in this process. If we accept therefore that every young person has the right to achieve standards of excellence and success at every level, then we as educators have an obligation to ensure that the adolescent is equipped with the skills to enable him successfully to negotiate some of the demands within this attainment process. The impending requirement for profiles of achievement highlights the need for formative consultation between teachers and students. One aspect involves study skills.

The inclusion of study skills in the curriculum concentrates upon the 'how' and not predominantly upon the 'what' of the curriculum experience. They encourage young people to take responsibility for their own learning patterns, so raising levels of achievement if the student considers the cost–benefits ratio of changes in his behaviour to be worth while.

When a young person moves along that fatalistic path which ensures that he fails to achieve success, he receives very strong messages from significant people in his environment that he is the failure. He then internalises this negative picture and we are left with a sad, despondent and underfunctioning youngster, who is on the receiving end of a curriculm response which has sold him short. We have a moral as well as a professional obligation to ensure that any young person has the skills which will enable him to unlock the curriculum so that he can positively participate in all it aspects. He cannot undertake this if he does not know how to study and what is available. A number of schools are now looking at the 'how' of learning and this involves the need to look at the processes of study.

A survey undertaken amongst a group of sixth formers demonstrated that many students had difficulties when faced with formal study demands. Whilst the reference is dated the sentiments remain the same: 'the difficulties mentioned were almost entirely confined to changes in the nature of and approach to work demanded, particularly in learning how to study on their own and how to organise their work without assistance' (Morton-Williams *et al.*, 1970).

A further study confirmed these findings. The conclusions of this NFER–sponsored research project covering 4,500 students was that there is 'need to consider in greater detail the provision made for reading/study skills in different institutions' (Dean *et al.* 1979).

There are a number of related studies which emphasise that study skills should not just be confined to the sixth form. They should permeate the whole of the secondary curriculum. It might well be that a core approach to study skills could be undertaken in the pastoral curriculum, with linkages from and to each subject/interest area, complementary to this core. A possible core outline may look like this:

Study skills – core issues

(1) *What are they?* What do I need to be a good student, or conversely, what is it which prevents me from studying effectively?

(2) *The environment of study* Where is the best place for me to study? Given the facilitative aspects and constraints of my environment, can I work with noise? Do I like working in a group, do I share resources? Do I use resources, such as teachers, effectively?

(3) *Organisation of study patterns* How well do I organise my study procedures? Do I plan a list of activities? Do I prioritise items? When is the best time of day or night for me to study?

(4) *Distinct skills of study* Active listening, note-taking, paraphrasing, essay/project writing, preparing for oral work, reading for learning, skim and speed reading, examination preparation.

Such an approach should then enable a larger number of youngsters to use as of right the general facilities available in school.

Part Three   Special educational needs – the pastoral process

The role of the tutor as the 'named person' is introduced. Additionally the integrative pastoral processes of group structuring, counselling, problem-solving, identification, assessment and recording are considered.

A case study is included which illustrates how these processes shaped the learning experiences of a group of 14-plus youngsters who had a wide range of special educational needs.

This part of the volume concludes with a detailed list of resources which have been found useful in the pastoral curriculum.

The role of the tutor in meeting special educational needs

The purposes of this chapter are to:

- consider the role of the tutor as the 'named person' in the pastoral response to special educational needs
- explore structural procedures which can shape group environments for youngsters with special educational needs
- suggest strategies which can contribute to this process.

THE ROLE OF THE TUTOR IN MEETING SPECIAL EDUCATIONAL NEEDS

'There is a priority for creating contexts and climates which will prevent needs before they arise, or prevent them from becoming unmanageable' (Sayer, 1987). This comment refers to the importance of the context of learning as a contributory factor in an individual's development. Variable factors shape and determine the learning climate. A key influence within the school situation is the tutorial role. Marland attempts to unravel the complexities of the tutor's role by describing three tutorial approaches which evolve as a result of a school's interpretation of a tutor's pastoral responsibility and capability (Marland, 1974). These descriptions illustrate how the role which the tutor assumes can change the focus of pastoral provision within the school.

The *tutor depressed* role, regularly practised in pastoral process one which was introduced in Chapter 2, places the tutor in a non-influential, passive position. His role is seen predominantly as an administrative one within the tutorial period which is often aptly referred to as 'registration'. The tutor takes the register, reads out messages, in a registration period which is largely unstructured. The session is regularly viewed as a 5–20 minute slot to be 'got over', before the real business of teaching begins, and this attitude is communicated to pupils who see the 'pastoral' period as boring, a waste of time, but 'good for a laugh'. The negative influence which this period so often produces exacerbates problems.

Figure 5.1   *A school's pastoral focus*

Tutor ascendant	Tutor neutral	Tutor depressed
Tutor has ready and full access to all information on pupils	Information mostly available on request	Tutor not trusted with much information on pupils
Tutor vital part of reception and induction process	Tutor told that new pupil will arrive	New pupils sent to join group without prior notifications
Subject teachers actually contact tutor in the first instance	Subject teachers sometimes keep tutor in touch but not regularly	Subject teachers always go direct to pastoral head if little else on
Letters home written by tutor on his own initiative	Tutor can suggest letter required	Tutor not shown pastoral head's correspondence
Tutor basically responsible for attendance, calling for help if needed	Pastoral head follows up absence queries	Tutor checks presence in register but no more
Tutor plays an advisory part in vocational and educational decisions	Tutor's assessment noted in writing	All careers advice centralised
Tutor present at all major interviews with parents, careers officer, etc.	Tutor told what took place	Tutor not informed of such interviews
Tutor's view solicited by senior staff when pupils seen by them	Tutor informed reasonably fully of action taken by senior staff	Summary action taken by senior staff (e.g. caning by senior master) without notification to the tutor
Tutor feels full strong responsibility	Tutor feels junior assistant in care process	Tutor feels mere register checker

Source: Marland, M. (ed.) (1974) *Pastoral Care.* Heinemann, p. 75.

The head of the pastoral unit is the one who absorbs selective information about youngsters but often, because of the sheer volume of this information, he can do little more than temporarily hold on to it. A punitive stance is taken towards youngsters, often for the sake of expediency, because given the unbalanced, occasionally self-induced workload, there is little time for a long-term preventative pastoral response.

The *tutor neutral* role regularly practised in pastoral process two is that undertaken by a tutor who is perhaps willing to become extensively involved in pastoral care but is given by the pastoral head an 'apprenticeship' or 'junior assistant' role, which does not allow the tutor to assume autonomous responsibility for his tutor group. Again, as with the previous role, the pastoral head takes the initiative, 'dealing' with and 'understanding' those pupils with learning and behavioural difficulties who, supposedly, cannot be helped in tutor periods. This gives little incentive to the tutor who wishes to participate because the head of the pastoral unit may be protecting his leadership and 'understanding' role.

In the *tutor ascendant* role the tutor is regarded as the key person in the pastoral framework. He is able to identify and meet the varied needs of pupils in his group and is the first line of referral in the school communication system. This tutoring role contains the following salient elements:

- the creation of an ordered tutorial environment in which learning can take place
- extensive surveillance of youngsters, using a variety of observational strategies
- identifying needs
- recording achievement
- recording and collating of relevant information about youngsters
- liaising with personnel e.g. other staff, outside agencies, peers, parents
- translating external demands for youngsters e.g. (a) choosing options, (b) interpreting school rules and (c) illuminating a negative situation in which the youngster played a key part
- involvement in individual and group counselling
- encouraging problem-solving and
- extending the tutorial experience by using the skills of tutoring within the wider mainstream teaching situation.

All of these elements elucidate how the tutor ascendant role can meet the very varied needs of pupils with learning and behavioural difficulties. This is done primarily by monitoring responses, identifying needs, taking preventative and remediative action, and by participating in guidance programmes which are allied to the demands implicit in ILEA's achievement aspects.

Sayer makes refreshing reference to the need to focus upon the idea of the 'tutor as the named person':

> 'Insensitive legislation can be prevented from forcing children into distinct management categories ... this can be ensured by confirming

the responsibility of the group tutor for each and every child rather than transfer 'named person' duties to a specialist department'.

(Sayer, 1987)

This has to be the thrust of the tutorial role. It is one which extends the concept of special educational needs introduced in Chapter 1; it also powerfully influences the development of a whole-school approach to special education.

It has been conjectured that whilst pastoral care did, and in many schools still does, adopt a peripheral curriculum position, current secondary initiatives contain salient elements of the pastoral process. Consequently pastoral care and the tutorial role are moving from the periphery of the educational endeavour to the centre stage in curriculum considerations.

The tutor who is effective in his tutorial work will also be effective in his teaching. The two activities are inseparable. This is the underlying perspective of pastoral process three, described in Chapter 2. To concentrate upon feelings, commitment and motivation is part of the professional task of the teacher. It is not, as is often the case, the professional task of the 'specialist' pastoral member of staff, or indeed the special-needs teacher, who so often becomes compartmentalised in their professionalised 'care' role. The co-ordinating role of the tutor places him within a whole-curriculum context – this is the hub of Sayer's exposition (Sayer, 1987); the tutor and teaching role becoming totally integrated. Of crucial importance is how each member of staff brings the caring, teaching and tutoring aspects of their role into every situation – determining how one person relates to another. Indeed, should we really be talking about tutoring and teaching? Both convey a view of a one-directional relationship. Perhaps facilitator is a more appropriate word, describing a learning context and climate in which all participants share related experiences.

ADOLESCENT NEEDS – TUTORIAL CONTEXTS AND CLIMATES

Implicit in many of the national initiatives is the demand for change in the processes of curriculum delivery whereby teaching aims will eventually centre around pedagogical issues instead of solely responding to subject needs. This development will demand a change in interaction patterns within the classroom: 'A teacher needs to be able to call on an extensive repertoire of teaching and learning methods ... sometimes the mode or process of learning has its own lessons, more potent than the formal subject matter of the lesson' (Schools Council, 1981). This 'potency' involves both the teacher facilitator and youngsters engaging in interaction patterns which are based upon the processes of active learning.

The teacher who is engaged in a whole-school approach to special educational needs has to have or acquire the awareness, ability and skill to use a range of techniques which will be appropriate to the diverse spectrum of needs found in the mainstream secondary classroom.

Engagement in active curriculum processes demands reciprocal forms of learning which have implications for the degree of teacher involvement within the learning environment. Figure 5.2 illustrates how both the passive and the active curriculum emphasis shapes the learning process.

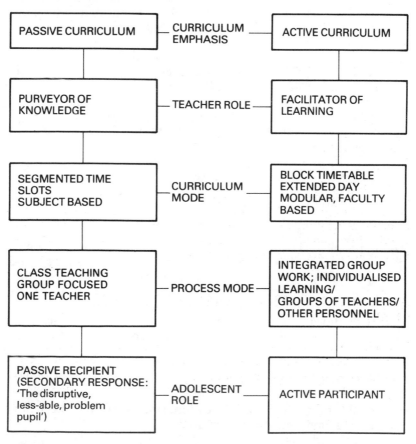

Figure 5.2 *Teacher and pupil involvement in the secondary learning process*

Through the medium of the passive curriculum, knowledge segments are 'given' to whole groups of youngsters which can result in the special educational needs of many youngsters being overlooked. The student, who passively soaks up knowledge, acquires the 'good and successful' pupil label. Those who cannot cope with this learning process often react with a secondary response. The teacher then categorises this response behaviour through the use of a number of labels – for example, 'disruptive', 'less able', 'distractible', 'lazy', 'thick', 'introverted', or any other label that seems appropriate from the teacher's viewpoint.

The active curriculum on the other hand enables youngsters to develop in an environment which encourages problem-solving. The youngster takes responsibility for her own learning under the guidance of the teacher facilitator. The learning environment is structured so that youngsters can engage in a range of developmental tasks which conceptually build on preceding ones.

STRUCTURING THE LEARNING SITUATION TO RESPOND TO SPECIAL EDUCATIONAL NEEDS

A number of studies of adolescent attitudes to teachers reveal interesting perceptions by students. There is unanimous agreement that a teacher gains respect by being:

> fair
> humorous
> strict and able to keep order, and
> approachable.

Young people feel comfortable in a defined situation within which they can learn. This defined situation has to be shaped and underpinned by a caring disciplinary framework which sets clearly known and predictable limits. A teacher who is aware of the special educational needs of youngsters is simultaneously conversant with those structural techniques which shape the learning climate, and which allow appropriate response to be made to needs.

THREE STRUCTURAL VIEWS

It is possible to identify three professional views which relate to how the learning environment is structured:

- **the passive structural view**

- the *laissez-faire* structural view and
- the active structural view.

Whilst these are oversimplifications, they permit the beginning of an ongoing analysis of the role of the tutor in meeting students' special needs.

The passive structural view

There is a view, often found in passive curriculum forms, which purports that a structured group environment demands an external imposition of standards. This structure suppresses unwanted symptoms and encourages young people to adhere unquestioningly to appropriate forms of behaviour. To deviate is to deserve punishment.

An example of practice

The tutor believed that adolescents were children in disguise and that they needed to be told how to behave. If they did not adhere to the standards defined by him, within his teaching room, then they would be punished through the imposition of detention or lines.

His tutor group would congregate outside his tutor room and would engage in overtly disruptive behaviour. Graffiti would be written on the walls of the corridor, litter would be dropped, horse-play would develop into more violent forms of behaviour. When the tutor turned the corner there were shouts of 'He's here', 'Be quiet, he'll keep us in', 'He's coming'. He would then bellow for them to stand in a straight line, which most of them did. A few openly rebellious youngsters would make a token gesture of defiance, but they too eventually would shuffle into line.

They would file into the tutor group, and stand behind chairs, waiting for the order to 'sit'. Some would be lolling over the backs of chairs; a chair would be pushed over; reprimand and stifled laughter would ensue; control would be restored and they would all sit.

The register would be taken, and then they were told to get on with something quietly, whilst the tutor prepared for the day's lessons. They were organised in rows facing the tutor. The majority of the group worked in silence. Some pursued their own activities – card playing under the desk, etc. Tom had a hearing impairment. He sat at the back of the tutor room away from the tutor. He was oblivious of what the tutor was saying and was regularly sent out of the room for misbehaving. He was either outside the room, which encouraged him to look in and make faces at the rest of the group, or if the misdemeanour was serious enough he was sent to the head of the pastoral unit, 'who will deal with you'.

The head of house would regularly then reappear with Tom, who had been cajoled into offering a bland apology to the tutor. He was then returned, apparently processed, to the tutorial session. It was only when a head of department expressed concern to Tom's mother that he appeared 'switched off' in lessons that his mother confided that he was totally deaf in one ear. Tom chose to sit at the back in defiance of his impairment.

The *laissez-faire* structural view

Ironically such a view does not accept that any organised structure is necessary within the tutoring/teaching situation. It is argued that to impose any form of structure upon an individual's search for meaning is to place restrictions on autonomous development. An alternative view could say that it is a negation of the educative role of the teacher.

One tutor believed that the education system was implicitly repressive and that it encouraged a conditioning of the individual to fit in with societal values and demands. He held the view that within his tutor room youngsters had to have the opportunity freely to express feelings and needs within a totally unstructured and uninhibiting environment.

He regularly arrived late, and the youngsters would be found running up and down the corridor, indulging in highly boisterous behaviour which was regularly accompanied by loud abusive shouting. When he arrived, laughter and occasionally derisive comments would ensue. Whilst he attempted to open the door, they would crowd and push around him. The tutor would deftly stand to one side as they tumbled into the room. Their desks were organised in haphazard fashion around the room.

Most of the youngsters who did sit at them sat with their backs to the tutor. Other youngsters aimlessly wandered around the room looking for an opportunity to relieve boredom. The first instruction from the tutor was regularly a plaintive 'Hey, be quiet!' which was always ignored. The noise eventually reached a level which bordered on hysteria.

The direction of communication was between youngsters – who shouted across the room and, even if they were sitting next to each other, had to shout to be heard. Some isolated themselves from the main group, and these occasionally had spasmodic contact with the tutor, who placed himself close to the wall at the front of the room. One very nervous and inadequate youngster was unmercilessly and subtly bullied. Consequently she truanted regularly. This enabled her to 'remove' herself from the tutor group.

Sally, when she was present in the tutor group, always sat on her own near the tutor's desk. He was quite oblivious to what was going on, cheerfully commenting, 'All right, Sal?' Before Sally could reply, his attention had flitted onto another area of disruption in the tutor group.

No task for students had been delegated as the tutor frantically gave out notices and collected in homework books (only a few were handed in). On some mornings he would leave the group for five minutes to get the register. One could deduce that this was possibly a period of calming respite for him. No set patterns of required behaviour had been articulated by the tutor. Consequently, upon his return the register was taken, still accompanied by noise and with the tutor shouting to be heard. Some pupils said they had forgotten their homework books. 'OK', replied the tutor, 'bring it tomorrow', but 'tomorrow' there would be no follow up. Six weeks into the new term many pupils had never had homework commitments checked. Other work commitments also had not been monitored and therefore many pupils were asking 'Why bother?' The tutor accepted that the noise level 'got a little out of hand' at times, but he had insulated himself from it.

Such a climate was damaging to all individuals within the group, including the tutor. It had a particularly unsettling effect upon those youngsters who had behavioural difficulties. It wound them up into a state of excited behaviour which often had repercussions in other lessons.

The active structural view

This view adheres to a belief that discipline must accompany self-growth. Individual development takes place within a number of interrelated social groups. The tutorial process, therefore, has to be underpinned by an awareness of responsibility for other people within the group situation. Such a facilitative learning environment does not merely happen, it has to be shaped. This involves the creation of a structured group environment which has known but flexible boundaries. These boundaries are adhered to through a process of responsible negotiation on the part of the individual within the group situation.

An example of practice

The group was allowed into the tutor room before the tutor arrived. The youngsters had a rota system for key collection enabling them to use the room for their own activities. The tutor often started the session with a joke, which elicited a friendly moan from the group.

It was a sign that he was on form and that he was the person with overall responsibility for group development.

The desks were organised on a friendship group basis and these sets of desks were loosely arranged in a semi/full circle. The tutor's desk at which he rarely sat was against the wall; instead he would situate himself in a central position in the group, moving from each desk cluster, sometimes sitting with a small group of youngsters. People moved around the room engaging in purposeful, co-operative activity.

The register, which was collected, again on a rota basis, from the office, was taken in total quietness. If a youngster was absent then more often than not one of the group knew the reason for absence. After registration the objective of the tutorial session was written on the board.

Most pupils started immediately upon their tutorial work, whilst a small group of pupils did various initial administrative tasks– collecting in homework, giving out information sheets, etc.–whilst the tutor dealt with immediate matters relating to specific pupils. He was totally involved in the tutoring process, projecting competence, reassurance and assertiveness.

On one occasion a boy, who was often disruptive and known to the tutor as 'the tester', started to pull a chair from under another boy. The tutor, who appeared to be aware of the movements of all pupils within his group, immediately saw the developing incident. With a signalling look towards the boy, he asked in a humorous but firm way, 'Are you *really* going to cause him an injury, Lenny?' Sheepishly the boy stopped the horseplay because he was very aware of the boundaries within the group, which had been formed over a long period of time. There were unwritten rules which everyone knew and generally kept because they felt that they had a responsibility for the smooth running of the group, and they were a contributory element to the prevailing discipline climate. These rules included:

- there must be silence when anyone else is talking
- the fabric of the room must be kept in good order
- each individual to be responsible for his own equipment–including tables and chairs and
- there must be general awareness in the group about the needs of specific individuals who may need extra support that day/week.

Weekly rotas were on display which indicated areas of responsibility for individuals in the group, for example, bringing the register, organising the worksheets, preparing the coffee! At the end of the session a discussion explored the following issues:

- whether or not the aim had been reached
- what had been the restrictive processes which had prevented the attainment of the aim
- what had been the facilitative processes operating
- had all group members accepted responsibility for the attainment of objectives implicit within the aim?

Roughly a quarter of the tutorial session was spent on this activity.

PHYSICAL ENVIRONMENTS

The physical environment of any learning situation makes a crucial contribution to the creation of a positive environment. Most schools have corridors. Often these are echoing, noisy tunnels which can foster anxiety and aggression. Witness a narrow school corridor on a wet cold day, with youngsters and teachers struggling in both directions to reach a room. The youngsters are carrying bags and coats because there is nowhere adequate to leave them. The teachers are carrying piles of books and are barking instructions to 'walk on the left'. Once reached, the room can be a haven, a welcoming environment. The room climate however is influenced by a number of physical factors. A notable one, regularly ignored in secondary schools is the wall display. This can reveal examples of youngsters' work at all levels and can convey to the group that the tutor cares enough about the efforts to display the results. The physical environment of many secondary schools however, conveys an initial damning message to visitors that it is a sterile uncaring place in which to reside.

One head of an art department reluctantly released examples of work undertaken by youngsters in his department, so that it could be displayed around school. When it did go on display the comments from many youngsters were illuminative:

'I didn't know that *you* could draw.'
'Yeah, that's Bens work, but he goes for remedial doesn't he?'
'Did you design that record cover that's in Jackson house room?'

The case study in Chapter 8 illustrates convincingly how the provision of a spacious, well-carpeted suite of rooms contributed to the establishment of a 'home base' which reflected a calm learning atmosphere much appreciated and valued by the youngsters working within it. The There is a reticence to display youngsters' work in secondary schools yet it performs a variety of highly positive functions which contribute towards shaping an environment conducive to successful learning in the following ways:

- it shows that we value the efforts of the individual who has achieved success
- it enables the group to share the experience
- it transforms a static, cold environment into an alive and warm place in which to work
- it conveys a message to the youngster who has produced the work that she is contributing to the aesthetic environment of the school and
- it gives her prestige and feelings of self-worth.

This feeling of pride in work achieved is vividly illustrated in Sue Johnson's case study. The youngsters were encouraged continually to display examples of work not only for display on open days but also because one key group activity was concerned with sharing strengths and achievements with each other. Jane was a very insular individual who attempted to conceal her feelings of inadequacy by nonchalantly attempting to be 'one of the girls'. She wore heavy make-up and participated as best she could in the usual boy/girl 'banter'. In spite of her attempts, she remained very isolated. She enjoyed art but was reticent about putting work on display, commenting 'Nobody wants to look at that!' as she quickly filed it away into her folder. The City and Guilds group did have an open day and Jane was encouraged to bring her work from home to display in an allocated area. The week preceding the event she spent every spare moment in the SRD mounting her pictures. Youngsters in the group started to help her and eventually Jane and some of her peers could be observed having natural, frank conversations about her work. Jane was able to reveal and talk about success and others shared in it.

NON-VERBAL MANAGEMENT STYLES

There are a number of techniques which many effective teachers use in the learning situation. For some teachers these are intuitive; for others, they are skills to be acquired consciously. These include tone of voice, directness of look, facial expressions, body stance, physical proximity, gaze span and the mapping out of territory. It is a selective list but they are techniques which teachers have used to survive in what can initially be a fairly hostile environment. It is stressed the 'Most experienced teachers insist that the teacher must, if he is to survive, define the situation in his own terms at once' (Hargreaves, 1972).

This means using a variety of techniques, some of them quite idiosyncratic. One colleague described her experiences upon meeting a fifth-year group of very disaffected, 'non-exam' youngsters for the first time. Many of them had regularly truanted, some had experienced suspension from school. She stood waiting in front of her desk for them to arrive. Eventually a noise echoed up the corridor and they all tumbled into the room, acting aggressively, threateningly, blocking her out, testing her. After a few chairs had been turned over they eventually found seats. Two of them put their feet up on desks, folded their arms, and waited for her to perform.

She was an experienced teacher, and her first response was to wait in silence for a few seconds. She then took an overview of the whole group and eventually focused upon the two who were leaning back defiantly in their chairs with their boots on the desk. She started to walk around the room, looking out of the window, looking at sparse wall displays, pacing around the back of the class, by which time many of the youngsters were becoming fidgety and anxious. One of the boys who had his feet on the desk started to whistle and bang one of his books on the desk. The teacher went up to him, bent down and quietly asked what the problem was. He was so surprised at her intervention and close proximity that he fell off the precariously balanced chair onto the floor. There was an anxious silence.

At this point the teacher swiftly moved to the front of the room and started to convey to the group her expectations about how they should come initially into the room. They listened quietly. It emerged during subsequent discussions with her that they had thought that she had knocked the lad to the floor, so gaining immediate control over one of the group leaders. In reality, he had been so embarrassed that he didn't bother to inform the group otherwise.

Of course such a situation is a highly subjective experience which fortunately yielded the right initial results for one teacher. But how do you communicate to other teachers the skills inherent in this 'withit-ness'? It is an elusive quality, an intuitiveness which is the kernel of a positive learning environment. However, some of its elements can be identified by the profession; they can be learned, at least by some teachers.

Strategies for use in developing the tutorial climate

Observing groups: a time observation grid

Break the session down into time segments. Observe what activities are taking place within them. Ideally, this needs to be carried out by an observer in the classroom, but it is possible for a teacher to compile his own observation grid. This resource can be used for observation of an individual child in addition to whole group observation. It can be used collaboratively by both students and the tutor.

Figure 5.3 *A time observation grid*

Participants	Beginning	20 minutes	20 minutes	Ending
Students	Completing homework	Listening to tutor	Small groupwork (discussion and writing). Some misbehaviour	Draw together discussion
Tutor	Settling in. Checking homework commitments	Address whole group	Moving around helping small groups	Summarising points of discussion on board
Parent	Standing, arms folded, observing	Sitting on desk top at back of room	Sitting with one child giving reading help	Helping a small group of children to summarise their discussions

Student perception exercise

The grid form in Figure 5.4 enables youngsters to consider influential role players within the group situation. Within a secure and supportive environment youngsters are sometimes able to extend the exercise so that they are able to articulate their concerns about individuals who may be disrupting the equilibrium of the group. It has to work at an unthreatening level. Conversely the activity can focus upon distinct strengths of individuals in the group.

Other aids and techniques

The use of photographs depicts the visual aspects of a learning situation; portrays distinct role players, the physical layout of the classroom and the tutor's physical presence within it. It is useful to give one youngster responsibility for the use of the camera for a period of time and then ask him to elaborate upon his findings to the rest of the group. Video recording is an effective observation process. It is expensive and initially potentially distractive, but it allows a close scrutiny of interaction patterns in the classroom.

Figure 5.4
Pupil perceptions of each other within the learning environment. (Based upon an idea used in Ongar School, first year tutorial work – Summer term 1979–80)

How do we react to different behaviour?

Pupils in your group behave towards each other in different ways. You may think of some as being rude, dishonest, helpful, lazy, bigheaded, friendly, etc. Divide into groups of four, discuss and fill in the diagram shown, showing how you think pupils might react to the types shown in the diagram.

e.g.

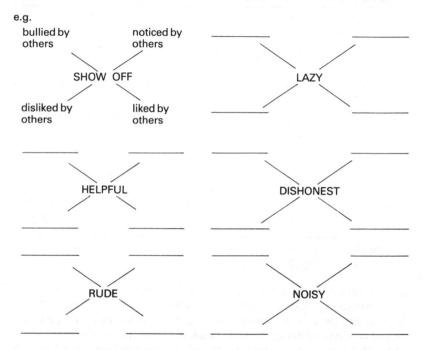

Discuss your answers with your *tutor*

Tape recording is a very useful aid as a method for analysing the learning environment. Tape recording aids:

memory recall
analysis of questioning techniques
identification of key talkers, including the tutor
assessment of group interaction techniques
pupil assessment of their contribution to the group climate.

6

Adolescent needs: counselling and problem-solving

The purposes of this chapter are to:

- consider the processes of counselling and problem-solving as an effective response to special educational needs
- suggest strategies which can contribute to these processes.

CONCEPTS OF COUNSELLING

In most of the current 14–19 secondary initiatives counselling assumes such importance that it has actually been included within the aims and objectives of a number of these initiatives. Counselling as a term has been loosely and ambiguously used over the years. People too easily and conveniently say that they are involved in a process of counselling when in reality they are engaging in processes of interaction which at their base are directive, judge-mental, repressive and instrumental in nature.

Counselling in schools and colleges has two major aspects. It can help individuals and small groups deal with crisis. This is an instance when a special need is dealt with–for example, a group of youngsters with severe learning difficulties who on a residential weekend broke into a farmer's barn, activated a harvester and could not really understand the consequences of their actions. Secondly it can be used by the teacher as a means of anticipating problems, exploring them, considering the options open to students with them and thereby increasing the probability that the students will be able to deal adequately rather than inadequately with the situation when it arises. For example, consider Sarah whose case study is described in Chapter 1. She needed the opportunity to articulate her concerns, to explore her social and academic development so that she could start to plan realistically her immediate future.

Counselling–a definition

Counselling involves learning about self and about how that self relates to other people. Gilmore affirms that counselling should help someone:

- cope more effectively with the business of being human
- live a more effective life
- answer the question 'What shall I do?'

(Gilmore, 1973)

The question 'What shall I do?' consistently accompanies the process of self-growth. For the adolescent who is striving to develop a positive self-concept it takes on a particular poignancy. For the adolescent with either a short-term or a long-term special need, this is especially true. Counselling assists in counteracting confusion and anxiety. It is a process through which people learn how to help themselves and in so doing they are able to answer the recurring question, 'What shall I do?'

This involves a process of change and a moving forward. It is the process which lay at the heart of the approach to special education described in Chapter 8. Most of the youngsters in this example felt that they had been rejected by a school system which focused upon weaknesses. Take, for example, the following comments:

'You have a problem with reading therefore you can't.'
'Your written presentation is dreadful.'
'You are not teaching that group are you?'
'Late again Lewis–I might have known!'
'You've been nothing but trouble since you came from that school, it's no wonder they kicked you out.'

They all convey very powerful negative messages about both individuals and the group. Youngsters reacted defensively in response to these comments. The immediate aim within the developmental learning environment was therefore to focus upon strengths, whilst emphasising that many youngsters had to accept responsibility for underperformance in a number of achievement aspects. Counselling both on an individual and a group basis helped us to work towards that aim. A useful loosening-up exercise ('Sharing strengths in a group', described at the end of this chapter) was used which encouraged a refocusing upon strengths rather than weaknesses. One group member, who had a history of being disruptive, pinned his strengths paper onto his bedroom wall and his mother, during an open day, brought it into school with her. She could not believe that these comments had been written about her son although she always knew he 'had a lot of good in him'.

Such a developmental process underpins those achievement aspects described in Chapter 1. It is the essence of a whole-school approach to special educational needs; there is nothing mystical about it.

Fiedler attempted to ascertain whether one could have an ideal helping partnership, which did not depend upon 'professional' therapeutic approaches to care: 'Helping relationships have much in common with friendships, family interactions, and pastoral contacts. They are all aimed at fulfilling basic human needs, and when reduced to their basic components, look much alike' (Fiedler, 1950). In response to Fiedler's investigations a range of therapists indicated that the key features of a helping partnership transcended the 'professional' response:

> an empathic relationship
> therapist and patient relate well
> therapist sticks closely to the patient's problems
> the patient feels free to say what he likes
> an atmosphere of mutual trust and confidence exists and
> rapport is excellent.

It is very difficult to differentiate between these features and a learning approach to special educational needs which has the individual at its centre.

Client-centred counselling

Carl Rogers, an eminent exponent of client-centred therapy, reformulated the concept of psychotherapy. He also asserted that at its essence it is a relationship between persons. He saw the salient prerequisities of any helping relationship being:

> congruence
> unconditional positive regard and
> empathic understanding

(Rogers, 1961)

Congruence

This is that quality in a relationship which conveys genuineness. A person is what he is. Professional barriers are replaced by genuine feelings which express that moment's experience. A person who is truly genuine does not have to shelter behind roles or labels. It is one human sharing an experience with another person.

Unconditional positive regard

Every individual has the need 'for unconditional positive regard. However, as teachers we regularly place conditions of worth upon the individual. For example, in the school situation we may implicitly suggest that we will only give someone positive regard if they fulfil certain obligations which will feed our needs.

if – you do your homework;
you wear your school uniform;
you pass your exams; or
you sit quietly and absorb what I am saying.
then I will give you positive regard, but it will be conditional upon how appropriately you respond to me.

A truly facilitative psycho-social environment encourages healthy, responsible growth. It allows the individual to explore alternatives freely within a caring relationship. We may not agree with an individual's behaviour but we will try to understand. In so doing we are facilitating exploration, experimentation and self-growth. We are allowing the individual to function more fully. Take for example the disruptive outburst in the classroom: we do not need to condone it and in so doing engage in collusive behaviour but we can attempt to understand the reasons for that behaviour.

Empathic understanding

This has been described as walking in another person's shoes, attempting to feel what it is like to be that person. Through the reflection of conveyed feelings, the helper reassures the youngster that she is not alone, and that a genuine attempt is being made to share feelings. It can only be an approximation, however, when we say that we understand. One person's experience is unique to that person. We can only speculate and share facets of that experience. From the client's viewpoint the exhilaration is in knowing that someone is at least making a genuine effort to understand, and is focusing totally upon you. It can be an enriching experience for both client and counsellor. A number of people are afraid of real honesty in communication. Powell observes that 'We would rather defend our dishonesty on the grounds that it would hurt others, and, having rationalized our phoniness into nobility, we settle for superficial relationships' (Powell, 1969).

Within the teaching profession some would defend the need for social distance by arguing that teaching is a risky and herculean task. We have therefore to maintain distinct distancing roles within the classroom: the teacher and the taught.

PARA-COUNSELLING SKILLS FOR USE WITHIN THE LEARNING ENVIRONMENT

There are a variety of para-counselling skills which can be effectively used within a structured learning situation. They are the base effective skills of the learning relationship, and are not the exclusive resource of the professional counsellor or pastoral carer.

Observation

Through the use of a whole range of senses it is possible to pick up communication cues from either the individual or the group which enable us to assess another's immediate disposition. Take, for example, the frustrated and potentially disruptive youngster who is becoming agitated because he is experiencing difficulty in a learning task. His actual body language – the tenseness, the distracted gaze, the drumming on the desk – are all behaviours which convey messages about that youngster which the perceptive tutor is able to identify.

Active listening

Active listening, giving a person time to communicate, is the pre-eminent helping skill. It facilitates positive communication.

An enhanced skill which most teachers have is the ability to talk, but one has to query whether they are as effective in their listening skills. Regularly young people articulate their concerns in response to the demands which regularly confront them. Through listening to verbally expressed anxieties we are able to pick up perceived needs.

In the school situation we can convey anxiety and disinterest to young people through ways in which we apparently listen. A youngster comes to us for help and we retort, 'Yes, yes, I know what you mean, you need to try a bit harder.' Simultaneously we are barking orders to other fourth year youngsters, with half an ear on what is being expressed. For example, consider the youngster who in science is being taught concepts beyond her capabilities. She has not done her homework and she is terrified of facing her science teacher. When we listen, and show it, we are confirming to young people that their words are worth listening to. Enhanced listening involves picking up the music behind the words. By listening – often to quite inadequate and stumbling words – we can tentatively try to reflect expressed feelings back to the youngster. Metaphorically, a mirror is held up to someone so that they can see their expressed feelings articulated by someone who empathises with them.

Open questioning and non-conforming statements

Regularly in teaching we use closed questions and statements which will shape and influence the kind of response which we wish to hear. Open questioning facilitates a freeing of verbal responses:

Maybe we could start off by you telling me what made you decide to see me about this ...
What do you think might happen if you ignore it ...
I want you to think back to a time when it wasn't like this–what did it feel like when you were going around with your old mates from Charley Street?
Is it just you and me who are involved in talking about this?
I don't fully understand, but I'd like to try and understand it a bit better.
What is it that has prevented you from talking to Mr Taylor about this?
It's becoming clearer to me, the picture I'm getting is that ... am I along the right lines?
From our discussion so far it appears to me ... what do you think you want to concentrate on?

Open and tentative questioning allows the young person to express feelings. Consequently it can enable an effective learning programme to be planned which is aware of articulated needs which have been freely expressed.

Summarising

This process involves gathering all the points together which the youngster has expressed. One is then able to isolate key issues which he may wish to focus on.

It is useful, for example, if a youngster is not very articulate, for him to use written, illustrative or diagrammatic summaries. To see a visual representation can help to clarify confusion. For example, one youngster had a history of school refusal. Through the use of a life-space diagram, illustrated in Figure 6.5, he was encouraged to

draw matchstick figures which indicated people who were significant to him. He put two specific teachers right at the edge of the
paper. It transpired that these two staff both intimidated him and
they strongly contributed to his fears about school.

Identifying themes

In many conversations specific themes can reoccur. It might be the
individual who is a victim, a bully, a loser. Through the counselling
process a specific theme can be isolated and reflected back to the
youngster.

'You said a few moments ago that you made fun of him when the
teacher was not looking; then you said you laughed loudly when
he fell of his bike in front of his mates. It seems as though there
could have been a number of occasions when you made him feel a
bit of a fool. Do you think that that may be one reason why he's
started to pick on you?'

Confrontation

This is one of the most difficult skills, and it has to be accompanied
by a high degree of empathy. The aim is to help the youngster to
consider issues which he is avoiding exploring. A youngster may
subtly try to persuade you to participate in collusive behaviour. He
has no intention of owning or facing up to the problem, but instead
attempts to induce you onto his side. In such a situation the only
honest response may well have to be caringly confrontational. This
is particularly true if the youngster is engaging in self-damaging
behaviour. There is an element of risk. To confront could elicit a
number of explosive responses, but if the relationship is based upon
empathy and positive regard, then these feelings can, in most
situations, be held. Peter, in Sue Johnson's case study, avoided
facing the fact that his loud, aggressive and physically intimidating
behaviour affected how people responded to him. His consistent
retort was that everyone else was at fault. By providing Peter with
concrete examples and exploring events leading up to that
behaviour he was encouraged to consider the consequences of his
actions upon others and upon himself. In that group environment it
was impossible for him to present excuses which he could play
upon. The group supported him but did not collude with him.

Task orientation and contract formation

We are involved with the current teaching situation and with those influences in a youngster's environment which impede progress towards the attainment of achievement. It is useful mutually to negotiate a simple contract in which the achievement goal can be indicated. All those people who sign their names on the contract are committed to helping the youngster attain that goal. Figure 6.1 illustrates a mutually formulated contract for use by a student who was continually arriving late to school.

Figure 6.1 *An achievement contract*

Goal to be aimed for:
Arrive on time for school

Tactics for achieving this:
1 Ask brother to reset alarm clock when he goes out on early shift.
2 Prepare all equipment for school the night before.
3 Stuart to knock on my door on his paper round.
4 Tutor to contact Mum if I'm regularly late.
5 Keep a time sheet for a month, indicating times of arrival at school.
6 Discuss schedule with all helpers.

Helpers' signatures:
Tutor   –   Mrs Taylor
Mates   –   Stuart
                    Wendy
Mother   –   Mrs Bosworth
Brother   –   Gary Bosworth

Signature: Gerry Bosworth

Gerry was not motivated to come to school because the commitment referred to in Achievement aspect 4 had been diminished through a series of negative school experiences. Additionally he shared a bedroom with his brother, who worked on early shifts at the factory. Consequently, after being woken by the alarm at 4 am, Gerry would turn over and sleep in. His mother, who slept in the next bedroom, also got up late to 'save electricity'. When he did arrive at school Gerry regularly missed the first part of the session, and was reprimanded by the staff. No one had attempted to ascertain why he arrived late, even though his termly report indicated that his lateness was a consistent practice.

Through the use of the contract he felt 'at least someone notices'. There was a pressure to change, but he had support through this process. Additionally the responsibility for change was his. He saw the reasoning behind it and the consequences of change.

Counselling skills within a group situation

Active and positive participation in group development is an essential part of the educative process. This interaction allows the individual to develop greater understanding, self-growth and self-acceptance.

The underlying objectives of both personal and group counselling closely correlate. However there are salient differences. The tutor has to have the awareness and competence to cope with these differences. Within the school situation the tutor needs an awareness of:

● structural group forms
● group assessment procedures
● individual observation techniques
● group dynamics and the individual allegiances
● patterns of behaviour
● the hidden 'agendas' which each member brings to the group, including the tutor
● those members who attempt to sabotage group activities
● those members who at some time need the privacy of not having to participate actively in group activities and
● a repertoire of group development exercises.

Within a safe and non-threatening group environment youngsters are then able to:

● assume responsibility for learning
● communicate effectively
● understand each other's points of view
● work co-operately together
● plan effective learning programmes
● work at their own pace
● mutually care and support each other and
● undertake peer counselling.

The case study in Chapter 8 illustrates the way in which a facilitative environment, shaped by the use of group counselling skills gradually enabled a youngster such as Richard to develop a positive view of himself. His severe epilepsy had a grossly disabling effect. he had formed a helpless view of himself–'I have fits and you have to help me.' Within the group he was encouraged to make a realistic appraisal of his own capabilities and limitations; in return his classmates offered their support during his seizures and their assistance when he experienced difficulties with his academic work.

During the field trip when he continually complained to members of his working party that he could not plant the saplings, Peter told him to 'stop complaining and get on with it'. He did!

The counselling elements of congruence, unconditional positive regard and empathic understanding were consistently worked for within this group. To work in this way demands energy and commitment; it also asks teachers in the school situation to look at how they organise themselves and youngsters.

PROBLEM-SOLVING

Dewey's (1966) axiom is that problem-solving or reflective thinking should, whatever the curriculum context, form the nucleus of the educative experience. His problem-solving process contains five cyclical stages as shown in Figure 6.2.

Figure 6.2 *Counselling and Dewey's problem-solving model*

Stage	The counselling process
Suggestion	Through reflection the learner becomes aware of the problem
Problem	The distinct problem is identified and made concrete
Hypothesis	A tentative hypothesis is made concerning how that problem can be solved
Reasoning	The potential consequences of the action are reasoned out
Testing	After careful consideration the hypothesis is tested.

This five-stage problem-solving model has close similarities to a three-stage helping model promulgated by Egan (1975).

A three-stage helping model

In this model Rogers' client-centred approach to helping is amalgamated with behavioural precepts (see Figure 6.3).

The basic thesis is that people can be taught to help themselves but they need the skills with which to do this, the kernel of effective pastoral care. The goal is upon action and experimental growth. The youngster in the learning situation receives empathic understanding and acceptance from the teacher, whilst simultaneously working out specific stages of action.

Egan likens life to a kind of battlefield in which the individual is struggling to live more effectively. He emphasises that the individual has initially to make a forcefield analysis of perceivable problems before he can begin effectively to move forward.

This initial process has similarities to Dewey's 'suggestion' stage. The tutor has to support the individual whilst she identifies and, in so

Figure 6.3 *A three-stage helping model, based upon Egan (1975)*

Pre-Attending
Attend to the other person physically and psychologically.

Explore
Stage one–responding/self-exploration
The counsellor responds to the pupil with respect and empathy. Gain background
information ('set the scene'). What will the contractual relationship be about? A
summary of the problem area to be explored. A difference between probing and
paraphrasing. The pupil, with support, tries to explore feelings and experiences.
Why is he/she living ineffectively.

Understand
Stage two–interactive understanding on the part of the counsellor
A piecing together of data; identify the problems. Try to get behind the words,
tentativeness. Make demands on the pupil:
(a)   express tentatively in concrete terms what is only implied
(b)   summarise core material–gather points which have been brought up. Use
      pictures if necessary
(c)   identify themes which keep coming up
(d)   try to develop a vague comment into specific statement
(e)   alternative frames of reference: 'What would it feel like if you did——?'
(f)   confrontation–an unmasking of games.

Stage three–action acting
A collaborative programme of action.
(1)   *Identify the problem*–the immediate need:
      (a)   state the problem in such a way that it appears solvable
      (b)   try to make the pupil 'own' the problem
      (c)   have the pupil state the problem concretely
      (d)   break the problem down into workable units.
(2)   *Establish priorities:*
      (a)   give some priority to pressing problems
      (b)   choose some problem, initially, which can be handled relatively easy
      (c)   choose a problem that, if treated, will bring about general improvement.
(3)   *Establish workable goals*
      Break down the goal into small units.
(4)   *Take a census of the means for achieving goals:*
      (a)   list all the restraining forces which keep the pupil from the goal
      (b)   list all the facilitating forces at work which help the pupil reach the goal
      (c)   underline the forces in each list which seem most important
      (d)   look at positive action steps for each underlined force which could reduce
            or enhance that force.
(5)   Choose the means which will most effectively achieve identified goals.

doing, 'owns' the problem. It is not then related to either the tutor's or
the school's needs but to the youngster's developmental needs.

Once the learning problem has been identified, the young person
states what the problem is in concrete terms. If necessary a simple
contract can be formulated and workable tasks established. The
youngster then works towards these goals. Consistent and constant
support is given by significant people within that young person's
environment. In individual counselling the special needs of the
client are identified, explored and ways of dealing with them

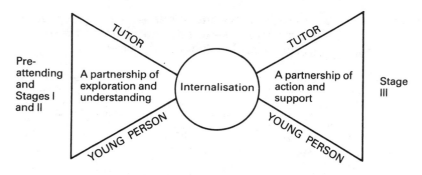

Figure 6.4 *The helping process*

considered. Thus counselling can meet many students' special educational needs.

STRATEGIES FOR USE IN THE COUNSELLING ENVIRONMENT

Sharing of strengths (one to one)

It is culturally not acceptable to talk about our personal worth. We typically show modesty by playing down our strengths. Many youngsters genuinely feel non-plussed when asked about their strengths, because in school we often emphasise weakness. The following exercise makes youngsters glow. Initially some boys refer to it as a 'cissy' exercise, until they experience being on the receiving end of positive comments about themselves.

Method

Split the group into twos. Ask each partner to talk for approximately one minute about the strengths of the other person, e.g. 'What I like about you is: the way you make people laugh, the way you look after your Mum, the way you stick up for people.' Interestingly this exercise encourages the receiving partner to practise concentrating upon listening!

Sharing strengths in a group

Following the one-to-one exercise it is profitable to develop this 'sharing of strengths' focus into a whole-group exercise. Discuss first of all how they felt in the one-to-one situation. Feelings of modesty regularly permeate this exercise. Stress that in our society we have subtly to disguise pride in our achievements.

- Encourage the group to focus upon self-achievements, 'I would like you to think about anything which you think you are good at. Would each person in turn finish the sentence, "I feel that I am good at..." ' People have to be allowed to opt out if they wish–a knock on the table indicates this. Hearing other people's expressions gives them permission to speak and regularly the process encourages them to participate. If someone is not able to participate then either the tutor or another group member states something positive about that individual.
- A concluding activity to this session could be for all group members to have a piece of blank paper pinned to their backs. Youngsters are encouraged to walk around the room and to write a 'strength' on a colleague's paper. At the conclusion of the session they can take these sheets with them as a record of the session.

Active listening

Very rarely do we genuinely and totally listen to what people are saying to us. The traditional teaching situation does not encourage this. In a tutor group, we are presented with opportunities for new modes of interaction. This exercise encourages individuals to focus totally on another person for a short period.

Method

In pairs, each person to talk for about two minutes on 'An important thing that happened to me', or 'Something I feel strongly about'. The partner, through eye contact and bodily posture, has to convey that she is genuinely listening to what is being expressed. She then reflects back verbatim the words which the person has used.

Eye contact

Eye contact is a very potent force. Witness the youngster who attempts to avoid the reality of a situation, or the one who feels that she is being unfairly treated and so avoids looking at the teacher.

'Look at me when I'm talking to you!'

She glares at her interrogator, then quickly escapes eye contact again.

A colleague of mine recently recalled an interview experience. One of the key interviewers, having asked a question, totally avoided eye contact with the interviewee.

Eye-contact avoidance can be a powerful ploy. It can, however, convey to the other person messages of disinterest, insincerity and avoidance tactics. A steady eye contact conveys empathy, understanding and genuineness. It is a similar process to active listening, but eyes have an additional and penetrating visual impact which communicate a range of emotions.

Reflection of feelings

Reflecting feelings back to a person indicates that we are attempting to try to understand expressed feelings. This can be a difficult exercise for some youngsters, but worth trying.

Method

In pairs. Each person to talk for a short time about 'Something that concerns me'. The other partner then attempts to reflect back to that person the feelings expressed, for example:

'I am concerned that when the time comes for me to leave school I will not be able to pass my exams because I haven't understood the work. This means that I won't get a job.'

Possible response:
You feel:

- very worried because you don't find the work easy
- anxious about your future work situation.

Alternative 'feeling' words

(i)   On the board, through a brainstorming process, list a few 'feeling' words, e.g. anger, love, hate, joy, sadness, pain.

(ii) Through the same process attempt to find synonyms for each word, e.g. *angry* – furious, explosive, displeased, irritated, inflamed.

(iii) In pairs, ask each partner to express a feeling in one sentence. The partner, using a synonym, has to reflect the feeling to the partner.

Problem-solving

Ask individuals to write a paragraph expressing a problem, personal, study skill, work, etc. Stress that this will be confidential, and that therefore they must not put their name on the paper. Ask volunteers to place their problems in a box. Consider each problem. (This can be a gradual process, one problem considered every session, depending upon the time element!)

- through discussion
- collating tentative suggestions for action on the board
- through the use of the third stage of the counselling model.

Incomplete sentences – self-expression

It is possible to encourage youngsters to talk about themselves through a format which can be structured around general or particular themes, for example:

'My friends think ——'
'My best friend is ——'
'I think friendship is ——'
'Friends easily ——'
'All of my friends are ——'
'Friendship is ——' and
'I get worried about friends when ——'

Additionally youngsters can be encouraged to make up their own sentences about themselves, or make up a list of incomplete sentences for someone else.

Self-description inventories

An inventory is a list of statements which someone is asked to tick so that one can ascertain whether a statement applies to them or not. There are numerous published inventories which can be used in group work. Alternatively they can be easily produced, e.g.

Like me   Neutral   Not like me

I tend to like being on my own.
If I find something difficult I stick at it.
I like to act the clown in the group.
I have a very short temper.
I like to be part of a crowd.
I like to work on my own.

Role play

The active nature of role play encourages many youngsters to lose some of their inhibitions. However if it is abruptly and crudely introduced it can produce anxiety. It is useful for a tutor initially to assume a role-play position to illustrate the process.

Role play enables someone to move in someone else's shoes, it helps to illuminate a social situation in a very succinct way. It can be used to practise appropriate forms of behaviour in potentially stressful social situations, e.g. in preparation for a work-experience placement or an interview situation.

It can illustrate to a youngster inappropriate forms of behaviour. Tracy had for a period of time, been stealing money from the couple for whom she 'baby sat'. Through a role-play situation she was able to observe her actions and in particular the consequences which her behaviour had for the young couple and herself.

Life space diagram

This is a very simple technique whereby the young person is encouraged to consider himself and his relationships with others. A youngster can draw matchstick figures and then talk about their importance to the central figure of 'Me'. This is a very informative exercise, particularly for the youngster. Through this placement process he is able to explore the importance of significant people within his life. The reasons for placement of those figures which are furthest away from them are sometimes worth exploring (see Figure 6.5).

Brainstorming

Every youngster is able to express a feeling, for example 'Happiness is ——' Responses are shouted out and freely recorded on the board. This process loosens inhibition; everyone has a go. It is a useful preliminary activity to the complete sentence exercise.

Expression of one feeling in the group

Encourages a sharing of feeling within the group. Each person in turn finishes the sentence, 'The nicest thing that happened to me yesterday was ——'

Physical self-image exercise

One issue which a number of young people are predominantly concerned with is that of physical self-image. This is particularly

Figure 6.5   *Life space exercise*

true for those youngsters who are physically disabled. There is a media emphasis upon physical attractiveness which puts an added degree of pressure upon a youngster who is attempting to come to terms with bodily and emotional changes.

This exercise elicits discussion and allows youngsters to loosen expressions of feeling on an issue about which they may feel self-conscious.

- From a collection of clothes catalogues, comics and magazines, ask individual youngsters to cut out pictures of how they would like to look. (Alternatively for those who might find this a threatening exercise, ask them just to choose three fashion pictures which appeal to them.)
- Ask them to discuss these with a friend, 'I like the way these people look because ——'.
- As a group exercise ask youngsters to brainstorm what they understand by the term 'physically attractive person'.
- Repeat the exercise using the term 'attractive personality'.
- Through an analysis of the two sets of the words attempt to

differentiate between those physical and personal qualities which contribute towards individual attractiveness.

Study issues

Ask individuals to complete a specific sentence on a slip of paper, e.g. 'I would be a good student but ——'. Collect the sentences in a box and read out a selection. Sensitively discuss the responses.

Study anxiety

Some of the reasons why students underfunction in school are connected with poor study skill acquisition. An initial study skill session therefore has to focus upon the creation of awareness amongst youngsters, that they can actually do something about underperformance.

- On a piece of paper ask them to list as many responses as possible to the question: 'What are some of the things which would help me achieve in school?'
- Put these in a box.
- Ask people in turn to take a paper out of the box and to read out some of the responses.
- On the board, which already contains a broad draft framework of study skills compiled by the tutor, collate the responses, for example:

  Skills I need for study
      the right place
      the right equipment
      people who will help me (including self-help groups)
      maintaining motivation
      taking notes
      essay writing
      reading for learning
      active listening
      memory training
      organisation processes (particularly before/after school and before/after sessions).

- Discuss in detail the value of study skills. They are not merely to help students pass examinations, they encourage people to explore life issues in a productive and effective way. They encourage inquisitive and exploratory thought which brings with it a sense of independent decision-making.

- Organise a programme of study skill education, prioritising areas. Initial ones might well be 'problem-solving', 'ideal places to study at home and at school'.

There is a danger that such a brief description of counselling techniques could distort and over-simplify them. The reader is encouraged therefore to explore further techniques by reference to counselling texts (some of which are given in Chapter 9), and additionally through active participation in training and development sessions for counselling.

Adolescent needs: identification, assessment and recording procedures

The purposes of this chapter are to:

- consider the processes of identification, assessment and recording
- suggest strategies which can contribute to these processes.

TRADITIONAL PROCEDURES WHICH IDENTIFY AND ASSESS ADOLESCENT NEEDS

Schools have consistently passed judgements upon young people that have radically affected their life chances beyond school and inflexible assessment and recording procedures have regularly contributed to the formation of these judgements. The use of formalised tests has, over the years, assumed a pseudo-scientific integrity within numerous schools. This belief is based upon the apparent objectivity of tests which, it is assumed, enable them to measure ability levels accurately.

It is conjectured that the ease with which they can be administered enables the teacher to grade youngsters rapidly into 'teacher appropriate' groupings. This process does not demand too much from staff who are having to balance the needs of the total group and the needs of the individuals. It is a clean and uncomplicated categorisation procedure which instantly produces unmovable goalposts at which the busy teacher may aim.

An illuminating review of almost two hundred tests widely used in schools confirmed what many people have believed for years: 'Many teachers construct their views of children on the basis of these inadequate tests ... some tend to believe the results against their own judgements because the tests appear objective' (Goldstein and Levy, 1984). This research seriously questions the validity and quality of certain of those tests which are frequently used in the school situation. Teachers are encouraged to focus upon the weaknesses of youngsters. The inference is that once weaknesses are identified, they can be alleviated by the teacher. If weaknesses are too severe then treatment is administered by the remedial department. If this department cannot treat the weaknesses then the young person is referred to outside agencies.

There are some youngsters who do need extra support, which may not be available in the school. However there are those youngsters who are labelled as 'problems' when in reality it may be the curriculum provided which is leading to underfunctioning and alienation.

Real ownership of the problem may rest with an extremely limited and iniquitous grading system which overlooks the diverse facets which make up the individual.

THE CHANGING NATURE OF IDENTIFICATION AND ASSESSMENT PROCEDURES

Traditional procedures of identification, assessment and certification have elicited consistent expressions of concern from a number of sources. In consequence attention is now being given to those forms of identification and assessment which are formative in nature, and which contibute towards a summative record of achievement. These formative procedures lie at the heart of the concept of special education introduced in Chapter 1. This emphasises that needs are dynamic and they change as the youngster develops. The Warnock view is that needs are 'seen not in terms of a particular disability which a child may be judged to have, but in relation to everything about him, his abilities as well as his disabilities–indeed all the factors which have a bearing on his educational progress.'

It is argued in this volume that formative identification and assessment procedures which are essentially cumulative in nature enable the teacher to consider the youngster 'in relation to everything about him'. Needs are articulated by the student and other significant people in his environment. The teacher is then able to pace learning in response to the developmental learning needs of the youngster. He is then more able to master basic learning steps and so achieve a degree of success. The summative record of achievement illustrates the sum total of a youngster's success patterns over a period of time. The DES policy statement lists four 'purposes of records of achievement':

(i)　*Recognition of achievement*
　　　'recognise, acknowledge and give credit for what pupils have achieved and experienced'.
(ii)　*Motivation and personal development*

'increasing their awareness of strengths, weaknesses and opportunities',
(iii) *Curriculum and organisation*
'identify the all round potential of their pupils and to consider how well their curriculum, teaching and organisation enable pupils to develop the general, practical and social skills which are recorded'.
(iv) *Document of record*
'a short summary document of record which is recognised and valued by employers and institutions of further and higher education'.

(DES, 1984)

It is very clear that these innovatory procedures have implications for the degree of teacher involvement in identification and assessment. They demand a wider participatory audience and they give focus to the need for youngsters to become actively involved in the process of identifying and assessing their own needs. Through the use of a variety of approaches which draw upon the contributions of a number of significant people in the young person's environment, both developmental and special needs are identified and assessed.

They can be responded to not only by the teacher, but by a young person's peers and other significant people, in the context of a supportive group environment.

Figure 7.1 *Negotiating achievement aspects*

	Key participants in process
NEEDS ARE IDENTIFIED AND ASSESSED	Self, teacher, peers nurture figures
NEEDS ARE RESPONDED TO IN THE SCHOOL SITUATION	Teacher, peer, outside agencies
THE YOUNG PERSON IS ABLE TO RESPOND TO THE DEMANDS	Self
STRANDS OF ACHIEVEMENT ASPECTS NEGOTIATED	Self with support of teacher, peers nurture figures
STRANDS OF ACHIEVEMENET ASPECTS BEGIN TO BE POSITIVELY MET	Self

Staff consistently have to ensure that information derived from identification and assessment procedures is used for the benefit of the young person. The strength of any caring environment is in its awareness of:

- the current needs of the individual and
- the appropriateness of when to refer for help outside the group.

There are some teachers who absolve themselves from responsibility for teaching many youngsters. They indulge in a process of constant referral without first making any attempt to identify, assess and meet needs. There are staff however who are afraid to refer a youngster because they see this as a reflection upon their own inadequacies as a teacher. Consequently, unless causing too much trouble, the child remains in a developmentally restrictive environment. Both stances militate against the growth of both the teacher and the taught.

Within the school there has to be the facility for any young person to receive help from a wide range or sources. Figure 7.2 illustrates a proposed system of referral for use in a school which was organised in strict academic, pastoral and special resource categories.

The key aims of the referral procedure were initially:

(1) to encourage communication and exchange of information between form tutor and subject teacher (Stage 1);
(2) to place the tutor in a key monitoring role;
(3) to encourage the head of department (academic) to assume responsibility for the learning processes and outcomes within her department (Stage 1);
(4) to encourage the heads of upper and lower school to assume responsibility for wider learning needs, through a positive process of liaison with both academic and pastoral staff (Stage 2); and
(5) to facilitate a concentration by the special resource department and remedial department upon comparatively severe learning needs (Stage 3).

The objective in each stage was for each member of staff to:

- identify the apparent problem and
- initially take responsibility for that problem and to indicate the action taken (see Figure 7.3).

It was emphasised that the problem could be solved or reconstrued at any stage.

REFERRAL PROCEDURES

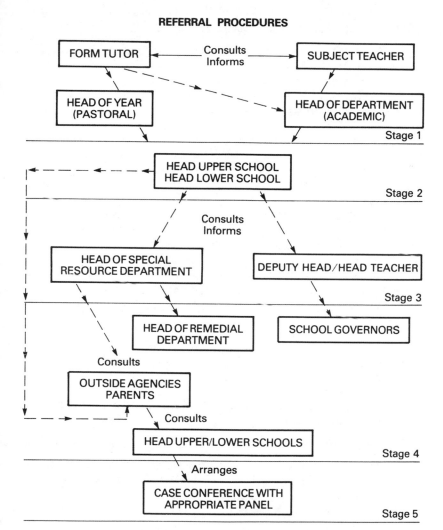

Figure 7.2

Industrial action by staff militated against the system's being comprehensively introduced within the school. Suffice to say that some staff were informally expressing initial concern about a proposed system of referral which would prevent the immediate placement of 'difficult' youngsters into the special-resource department.

The prime purpose of any structured referral system is to ensure that young people receive appropriate help to meet identified needs

Figure 7.3 *Referral and record sheet for children with potential special educational needs*

1st 1. DEPARTMENT (PASTORAL/ACADEMIC)...
Stage 2. GROUP (i.e. tutor group/set) ....

       3. DATE..

       4. NAME OF CHILD ....

       5. NAME OF PERSON REFERRING ....

       6. APPARENT PROBLEM...

            ....

            ....

            ....

            ....

       7. ACTION TAKEN..

            ....

            ....

            ....

            ....

            ....

2nd HEAD OF DEPARTMENT (PASTORAL/ACADEMIC) ....
Stage ACTION TAKEN ....

        ....

        ....

        ....

        ....

        ....

3rd HEAD OF LOWER/UPPER SCHOOL ....
Stage ACTION TAKEN ....

        ....

        ....

        ....

        ....

        ....

4th HEAD OF S.R.D ....   DEPUTY/HEAD.............................
Stage

      ACTION TAKEN ....   ACTION TAKEN ....

      ....

      ....

      ....

      ....

      ....

at crucial stages in their school career. This has implications for staff development and resourcing. Staff have to analyse and 'own' the learning environment from which the problem was referred, acknowledging that the problem could be outside the school's control. They additionally need to be aware that special educational provision to meet identified needs is the initial responsibility of every teacher.

Owning this responsibility is central to productive teaching. Teachers have to stay with the developmental needs of the youngster and pace learning accordingly. Any other programme response is inadequate.

Assessment is reciprocal; it has to be underpinned by educative processes which have at their heart the principles of counselling and guidance, which express care for students and staff within the learning environment. Balogh's study on profiling reveals that there is no universal criteria for what should be included in a record of achievement (Balogh, 1982). However, in an attempt to help schools identify what could be included on records of assessment, an overview of current profiles was produced for a Schools Council project (Goacher, 1983) – see Figure 7.4.

It is a comprehensive list which reflects the salient facets of ILEA's four achievement aspects:

   (i)   written expression, memorisation of facts
   (ii) practical application of knowledge
   (iii) personal and social skills
   (iv) motivation, commitment and self-confidence.

If schools are in the business of professing and practically implementing a whole-school approach to special educational needs, then it follows that this recording process has to be for all students. In the policy document, the DES states: 'Most young people leave school after eleven or more years of education with no comprehensive record of their educational achievements' (DES, 1984). This refers to those young people who have not gained traditional examination passes.

It is increasingly apparent that formative assessment procedures will be the mainstay of assessment in pre-vocational courses. The question is: will these become merely an adjunct to academic examination procedures?

The DES stresses that the summative record of achievement will be given at the conclusion of compulsory schooling and that it will be for all students. The timing of the receipt of the certificate however means that only a small part of the work carried out for external examinations will be recorded, because external examina-

Figure 7.4 *An outline of the material included on existing records of achievement, June 1981*

Section   *Possible items* (these items may be further subdivided)

A *Basic skills*
1 Language
    (a) listening   (c) reading
    (b) speaking   (d) writing

2 Numeracy
    (a) accuracy   (d) graphicacy
    (b) calculation   (e) 3-dimensional structures
    (c) measurement

3 Study skills
    (a) remembering   (f) summarising
    (b) presentation   (g) report writing
    (c) ordering/classifying   (h) location of material
    (d) note taking   (i) working alone
    (e) planning   (j) group work
                       (k) discussion

B *Personal characteristics*
    (a) attendance   (k) perseverance
    (b) confidence   (l) questioning
    (c) co-operation   (m) punctuality
    (d) co-ordination   (n) relationship/peers
    (e) concentration   (o) relationship/others
    (f) effort/enthusiasm   (p) reliability
    (g) initiative   (q) self-discipline
    (h) leadership   (r) self-motivation
    (i) open-mindedness   (s) self-reliance
    (j) originality/creativity

C *Life skills*–general
    (a) problem-solving   (d) co-ordination
    (b) trainability   (e) practical skills
    (c) adaptability   (f) safety-consciousness

  Life Skills–specific
    (a) use of hand tools   (e) form completion
    (b) use of power tools   (f) sign recognition
    (c) use of domestic appliances (g) work experience
    (d) use of telephone   (h) use of scientific/technological language

D *Personal achievements*
    (a) inside school   (b) outside school

  Dimensions not included above
    (a) visual skills   (d) understanding society/work
    (b) artistic ability
    (c) common sense   (e) health/physical ability

Source: B. Goacher, *Recording Achievement at 16+*, (1983) Longman for Schools Council.

tion results will come after the youngster has left school. How then can the two be combined? Are we going to have 'vocational certification' for the less academic, and 'academic certification' for the more able? The record of achievement has to be a key component of certification. Broadfoot stresses this: 'The record of achievement or student profile will not get the status it deserves unless it either comprises the certificate itself or is an integral and major part of the certification process' (Broadfoot, 1986). There has to be accreditation by outside bodies to give records of achievement credibility, otherwise their lack of status will ensure that they are a form of 'secondary modern' certification for a distinct group of youngsters who have followed a vocationally orientated, practically based form of curriculum.

FUTURE DEVELOPMENTS

The DES has encouraged the development of pilot programmes. Nine local authorities are participating in the scheme which is being monitored by national evaluators, who in turn report to a national steering group. There is the hope that towards the end of 1988 guidelines for the development of records of achievement which draw upon the experiences of the pilot schemes will be introduced to all schools for all youngsters.

In addition to these schemes a number of regional and cross-institutional schemes are being developed. The dilemma which is currently facing all staff in secondary schools is how to make sense of a plethora of initiatives which demand a radical change in both management and curriculum perspectives and which have implications for resourcing and staff development needs.

STRATEGIES FOR USE IN IDENTIFICATION AND ASSESSMENT PROCESSES

These identification and assessment process are an integral part of a whole-school approach to adolescent needs which is permeated by the values and techniques of the pastoral curriculum. Chapter 4 considered the developing role of the tutor whereby the tutor and teaching role become integrated in a whole-school response to needs. The question was posed, 'Should we really be talking about tutoring and teaching?'

The techniques which can be used in identification and assessment procedures are the essence of good teaching. They focus upon needs, they pace learning, they shape the curriculum and more importantly they enable a relevant response to be made to adolescent needs.

Diaries

Diaries encourage students to record feelings and observations over a period of time. They are not mere factual accounts but expressions of attitudes and feelings. It has to be stressed that the diary belongs to the youngster and that it is under that youngster's control.

Additionally it is sometimes useful for a tutor to keep a simultaneous diary in which she too records her feelings and observations about her relationship with particular youngsters. This latter exercise needs to be undertaken in an environment of care and trust. It should then be possible for the tutor and a particular youngster to compare diaries, and to reflect upon their observations about the dynamics of a social situation in which they are both involved.

Shadowing

Encourage individual students to ask a friend to shadow them over a period of time. Then the student will receive continuous and immediate feedback from the shadow as the action occurs.

'Me in school'

There are other conceptual frameworks in addition to this 'self' exercise which can be more closely related to the ILEA four achievement aspects. However this is a useful exercise to use with a new group. It was an exercise used very early on in Sue Johnson's case study and gave a useful overview of the wide range of youngsters within the group (see Figure 7.5.).

Ask the student to tick the appropriate box–'True', 'Not true'. Through the use of the sequence of counselling skills, ask her to elaborate upon her answers. For example, take the statement 'I think most lessons are boring. (True)'

Reflect feelings back to the student: 'It seems as though you are saying that school is uninteresting and a bit of waste of time. Can you think of one particular lesson where this is true?' 'How do you feel before the lesson?' 'Do you take these feelings into the classroom?' 'How would you like the lesson to change?' 'Which are some of the interesting and useful lessons which you go to?' 'What is it which makes these different from the rest; for example, what are some of the good things about geography?'

'The good things about geography are : ——.'

Figure 7.5 *'Me in school'*

	TRUE	NOT TRUE
1 I always try to present my work neatly		
2 I think most lessons are boring		
3 I never really listen to what the teacher says		
4 I am always mucking about in class		
5 If I do not understand I will ask the teacher		
6 I find a lot of lessons difficult to understand		
7 I am not quite sure what examinations I will be sitting at the end of the fifth year		
8 Teachers are always getting on at me		
9 I always take notice of what the teacher writes in my book		
10 I like joining in discussions		
11 I always try to answer the questions in class		
12 I daydream quite a bit		
13 I always talk with my mates in class		
14 I generally enjoy school		

'The person I am'

This activity asks the student to complete sentences about himself which he then discusses with someone else (see Figure 7.6.). Complementary and developmental activities could be:

- *An autobiographical writing* whereby he writes an extended paragraph using the sentences as a framework.
- *A testimonial* whereby he writes a testimonial about himself either for work, community service or further/higher education. Information is taken from the scale but slanted towards the potential testimonial audience.
- *A strip cartoon.* 'A Key Day in the Life of'. Through the use of a range of media, collage, drawings, painting, matchstick figures, the youngster produces a strip cartoon of a particular day's activities.

Figure 7.6   *'The person I am'*

Complete these sentences

1   My favourite things are——

2   It always happens when——

3   ——makes me sad

4   I would like to be able to——

5   I get fed up when——

6   Why is it that——

7   ——makes me worry

8   If only——

9   I think brothers and sisters are——

10   Girls in my group say——

11   I want to——

12   I am the kind of person who——

13   They always say that I——

14   I am good at——

15   ——is good for a laugh

Figure 7.7   *Am I satisfied with myself?*

You should have found out quite a lot about yourself and the picture you give to others. There are probably some aspects of you which could be improved with a little effort and thought.

List below any improvements which you think could be made or any changes that you would like to see.

(i)   e.g. I could improve my homework by taking more care over its presentation.
(ii)   I could arrive at lessons on time if I didn't waste time messing about with my mates.
(iii)
(iv)

- In a small group discuss ways of making improvements.
- Isolate one area which could be worked on.
- Set yourself a number of small targets over the next four weeks which could help you improve in that area. At the end of that period you will be asked to comment on your success in improving *you*.

Figure 7.8 *How am I doing?*

Work in pairs as you complete this questionnaire and you may be able to suggest
steps of improvement to your partner. Your form teacher may wish to discuss
certain aspects of your work with you individually.

1 During lessons I like it when ....

2 I do not like it when ....

3 I get really worried when ....

4 I was frightened when ....

5 I feel that I am getting on well in the following lessons ....
   ....

6 I feel that I am falling behind in the following lessons ....
   ....

7 Do you always understand what the teacher says in class? ....

8 Do you sometimes not understand what the teacher writes on the board? ....
   ....

9 Can you write easily and neatly, or is writing difficult? ....

10 When you write notes in your book is it easy–difficult–just alright? ....

11 Can you work out the maths examples? ....

12 How did you get on with your spelling? ....

13 How did you get on with writing essays? ....

14 Do you have difficulty in drawing, e.g. maps, illustrations?

15 Do you make contributions to discussions in class, or do you find this
difficult?

....

Summary
Are there any of these things you wish you could do better? Write them in the
order that you wish them most strongly:
1
2
3

- *'Am I satisfied with myself?'* (Based upon an idea developed at
  Ongar Comprehensive 1979–80 – see Figure 7.7.)

This exercise is designed to encourage youngsters to articulate
concerns, to encourage them to look for ways in which they can
improve attainment levels.
'How am I Doing?' (Taken from Lea House Form Booklet, Ongar
Comprehensive, (1979–80 – see Figure 7.8.).
In pairs ask youngsters to discuss their self-assessment sheet.
This sheet can then usefully be used as the basis for an individual
counselling session.

'Issues which concern me in the sixth year'

The aim of this exercise is to encourage students to look at the
constraining forces in their school career, then to look at ways in

Figure 7.9 *Issues which concern me in the sixth year*

Discuss these two questions with a friend and then record your findings.

1. What are some of the things which are stopping you performing satisfactorily in school?

```
```

2. What preventative action could you take? (List all the facts which could help you in this task.)

```
```

which they could prevent underfunctioning by listing the facilitative influences in their environment. Although this was used with the sixth form, it can be readily adapted for younger age groups and individuals (see Figure 7.9.).

Achievement aspects

An exercise which encourages a young person to stand outside distinct timetabled curriculum areas and to focus instead upon a wider self-view. Based upon Goacher's outline of records of achievement material (Figure 7.4) (see Figure 7.10.).

Figure 7.10   *Half-year report*

You are now almost half way through your fourth year. Look at yourself, and try to write *your own* report.

My report:

Area of development	*Achievements* (the standard which you have reached)	*Effort* (the work which you have put into reaching that standard)
Example		

1   *Basic skills*
    Language
    Numeracy
    Study		

2   *Personal characteristics*
    Confidence
    Concentration
    Initiative
    etc.		

3   *Life skills*
    General: problem-solving
                    practical skills
                    etc.
    Specific: form completion
                    etc.		

4   *Personal achievement*
    Inside school
    Outside school		

5   *Dimensions not included*
    Artistic ability
    Common sense, etc.		

In the achievement column mark yourself 1 to 5, and in the effort colum mark yourself A to E.

Imagine that you are your tutor; look at the grades which you have written down for yourself and try to write your own report, on yourself.

Half-yearly report on (name) ....

Discuss this report with a friend

Discuss this report with your tutor
Discuss this report with someone at home
Please make a list of (the things which I need to concentrate upon for the rest of the year):
-
-
-
-
-

—8————————————

A case study: 'Meeting adolescent needs–a developmental curriculum for 14–15 year olds'

*Sue Johnson**

THE BACKGROUND

The school was set in a small rural town and had within its student population youngsters from service families. Within the school there was a Special Resource Department situated in a pupose-built suite of rooms, described as a 'Resource Room Model'. This resource was designed to develop as an integral component within the curriculum organisation of the school. It aimed to maximise the degree of integration of children with special needs into the mainstream curriculum.

My arrival as Head of the Special Resource Department coincided with the teachers' industrial action of 1984 and the publication of a school report by HMI. These facts are relevant because ironically they were both contributory factors to the decision to introduce a City and Guilds Foundation Course as an option on the third-year course form. Whilst the HMI gave a positive appraisal of the 'caring and concerned' attitude of the staff working within the department who 'offered a wide range of skills, experiences and specialist insights', it drew attention to the existence of a few fourth- and fifth-year youngsters who were engaged in an option group of a more supportive context. In reality, these youngsters were being accommodated within the department because there was no cohesive provision offered for them within the context of the mainstream upper-school curriculum.

THE LEARNING ENVIRONMENT

The formalised upper-school curriculum with its emphasis upon subjects and traditional assessment modes was an inadequate

*Formerly Head of a Special Resource Department.

curriculum response for a number of youngsters, some of whom had learning difficulties and others who had revealed disruptive behavioural responses. Many youngsters consequently arrived in the SRD through an *ad hoc* referral process.

Internal referrals, mainly through the English or maths departments, seemed to identify the SRD as a remedial extension to their own departments and did not envisage the imminent return of their pupils to those departments. The educational response of the SRD was therefore to encourage heads of departments to become more actively involved in monitoring and providing for the special needs of children in the learning situation. Some children may have needed to have been withdrawn temporarily, but the focus was to be returning the youngster to the classroom as soon as possible.

Other than informal discussion in the staffroom, prevailing industrial action blocked channels of effective communication between departments, so essential to the consultative support role which I envisaged as being the underlying tenet behind the response of the SRD. The Foundation Course was therefore introduced rather as an expedient, hurriedly implemented in an attempt to respond to a variety of needs which, although not clearly defined, were known to exist for a number of third-year youngsters who would not be catered for within the official option structure as it then existed.

THE CITY AND GUILDS FOUNDATION COURSE

The Foundation Course was a programme of full-time education, based on a study of related groups of occupational and industrial activities, which was designed to provide an experiential route for young people approaching employment or specialised vocational further education. There were five schemes published by the Institute and the scheme in operation at the school was 'Community Care'. The aims of the course were:

1. to introduce students to careers and jobs and a knowledge of their implications for individuals throughout their working lives;
2. to provide experience in a range of occupational activities so that students can explore their interests and abilities and make a choice of vocation;
3. to give insight, knowledge and understanding of the nature, purposes and procedures of the community services;
4. to give an understanding of, and practice in, those mathematical skills which will be required by the student in the community and at work;

5. to develop practical skills;
6. to develop interpersonal and communication skills in situations likely to be met after school;
7. to provide an appreciation of the environment, the value of natural resources, and the need for conservation; and
8. to contribute to the development of social and leisure skills and personal qualities.

The scheme was based on two years of study during the fourth and fifth years and was allocated ten 45-minute periods per week which was equivalent to a double option and allowed youngsters opting for the Foundation Course to select two further subjects from the mainstream curriculum. The component headings indicated areas for assessment and examinations, although within the teaching programme these were integrated:

1. industrial, social and environmental studies;
2. community care skills and practice;
3. community care theory and science;
4. communication studies (written and spoken communication, numeracy);
5. careers education and guidance;
6. optional activities.

Coursework was compiled in a file and subject to continual assessment which was reinforced by an internally devised half-termly profile system. Communication Skills and Industrial, Social and Environmental Studies were assessed by examination and grades were awarded: Distinction, Credit, Pass or Fail.

Staffing

The staffing of the course was an important consideration which incurred some difficulties initially. The curriculum aims of the Foundation Course were synonymous with the experiential learning model and the ability to assume a facilitative role requires different skills and qualities from those where the teacher is directive. In addition, this kind of curriculum development requires co-operation in both planning, resources and delivery. This need for greater integration between teachers in planning the course posed a difficult problem at a time when industrial action was at its worst and staff morale was low.

A lecturer at a local higher education institution at that time became involved in development work within the course. She spent one full day a week in school, working with myself,

staff and youngsters developing and evaluating the programme.

The pupils

At the onset it was emphasised that the Foundation Course should
not be viewed as as an 'easy option' or an 'alternative' curriculum
form for the less able or disruptive youngster. Whilst it was
anticipated that the course would 'pick up' youngsters with
difficulties, in order to achieve credibility as a desirable and valuable
curriculum component, it must be offered across the ability range.
Ultimately the course picked up not only those youngsters who
were continually being referred for 'disrupted' or 'disaffected'
behaviour but also those youngsters who for most of their school
career had been quietly underachieving; a fact which was later to be
freely admitted by the young people themselves.

Unlike previous provision for these twenty youngsters however:

- the final decision to join the course was their own
- the aims and objectives of this course were clearly laid down;
  and more importantly for the youngsters
- offered them a qualification which had credibility with employers and
- in their own view, offered them equality of opportunity
  comparable to their academically more able peers, thus enhan-
  cing their feelings of self-esteem.

Brief pen sketches of six of the youngsters with a wide variety and
degree of special needs are given to illuminate the ways in which the
use of group learning skills led to a consideration of possibilities and
alternatives which helped them to see themselves as unique
individuals with valuable contributions to make to their own
learning.

Richard

Richard, having been diagnosed as epileptic early in his school
career, had gradually deteriorated throughout his secondary
schooling. On 'good' days Richard was literate, numerate, articulate
and able to achieve simple tasks in the classroom. On his
increasingly severe 'bad' days, he was almost continually comatose.
His speech became slurred and confused and his short- and
long-term memory were impaired for sometimes considerable
periods of time. He consequently lost his way around school, could
not remember where he was going and frequently lost belongings.

He was particularly unable to make satisfactory peer-group relationships. His peers partly believed him to be 'putting it on to get out of things', and he preferred to mix with adults upon whose sympathies he had come to rely and indeed on occasions, abuse. His own response to peers was negative. He had no friends and endured almost total isolation.

Susan

Susan was a bright gregarious youngster whose obvious awareness of contemporary issues made her a lively participant in the group. She was popular with her peers and, whilst at times domineering, displayed considerable leadership qualities. Susan enjoyed a very close and loving relationship with her mother whom she regarded as her 'best friend' and with whom, in the absence of a father, she shared increasing decision-making and personal confidences.

Whilst Susan's academic abilities were above average and she acknowledged the necessity to obtain 'good qualifications', she felt that the school had let her down because 'it doesn't teach you about the real world' and 'you're not allowed to say what you think'. Sadly for Susan, she did say what she thought, giving her a reputation amongst teaching staff for irreverent, disruptive behaviour which contributed to her placement in low-ability groups and subsequent alienation from school.

John

Academically, John was an intelligent, artistically creative and unusually perceptive youngster whose argumentative questioning and inevitable retort, 'But why?' contributed to his 'disruptive' label and his subsequent placement in low-ability groups, offering him little stimulation or motivation to succeed.

During his early childhood John had found himself defending his mother against violent attacks from his father. Now that she had separated and recently remarried, his relationship with his mother was intense and John protected their privacy with a fierce loyalty which excluded anyone else. His relationships with peers were strained. He made acquaintances to suit his mood but avoided close friendships and refused to be part of any group. The self-contained image John was attempting to adhere to often resulted in loud, aggressive and self-opinionated behaviour which made him unpopular with peers and staff alike.

Jane

Jane was the eldest child in a large family. She had younger brothers attending the school, to whom she never spoke but for whom she was responsible in the evenings when her mother went out to work. Her physical appearance was pale, she suffered from poor hygiene and was always tired. Jane was a sullen youngster who would only speak when spoken to, if then. She made no attempt to make friends and appeared to regard any overture of friendliness as an intrusion. She appeared not to have any sense of humour and would occasionally burst into tears whilst sitting quietly at her desk. On these occasions she would refuse to offer any explanation or accept any sympathy from concerned onlookers. She either absorbed herself in her work, which was usually thoughtfully presented, or 'switched off' completely. She was unable to accept even constructive criticism, usually responding with sulks and groans.

Peter

Peter had come, labelled 'disruptive', from another comprehensive. He would have liked us to believe that he had been moved because he had violently attacked a member of staff. The reality was that having exhausted one school's resources it was felt that he might benefit from a fresh start in another. Peter presented a disagreeable facade. He took on a tough, streetwise, aggressive, anti-school exterior, having convinced himself that if one school couldn't cope with him, this one certainly was not going to. Peter's home life had been very unsettled: he would spend some time with his mother and some with his father, but more often than not he lived with his grandmother who had provided him with the little security he had experienced. She had acted as intermediary on his behalf during frequent family disagreements. Peter's feelings of social and emotional insecurity coupled with his negative school experience reinforced his unpredictable and often immature responses, making him a potentially disruptive influence on the group.

James

James was conspicuous by his absence. It took us some considerable time to get to know him: he rarely arrived usually because, according to the other youngsters, 'He's overslept again' or 'He's with Mr X, Y or Z because he did this that and the other, yesterday.'

When he did arrive, James appeared older than his fifteen years. He was tall, good-looking and quietly assertive in his presence. His continual late arrival to school was in part due to his domestic responsibilities. His preoccupation with severe domestic difficulties coupled with an inability to concentrate on school work and painfully slow output negated any academic achievement he was capable of attaining. His dissentient attitude provoked a confrontational response from staff to which James could respond with uncontrollably aggressive behaviour, earning himself a reputation for disruptive behaviour throughout the school. He was, however, popular with his peers who appeared to regard him as a kind of hero, his arrival at the lesson inevitably arousing a cheer and an excited enquiry: 'How did you get on with old so and so?'

Discipline

The necessity to provide a well-structured learning environment was more than evident during the first few weeks of term when, having discovered that the faithfully promised 'base room' had been transformed into a long procession of demountables, we scrambled from one to another between lessons. Trying to maintain any semblance of order during these sessions was too often hampered by the whole-school crush which the sound of the bell seemed to signify. Waiting to gain admittance to our next venue in the confined space between twin demountables whilst still clutching open textbooks, sheets of A4 paper, rulers, pens, bags, PE kits, coats and umbrellas, tried everyone's patience to the limit–supplemented as it was with the occasional aghast comment from parting colleagues, 'You haven't got this lot have you?' or 'Obviously not the A-Level group!' Comments which were intended to be vaguely humorous, sympathetic overtones for the plight of the involved staff, but which did precious little to boost the morale of the youngster in whose earshot they were made.

Having finally gained entry into a classroom the tedious process of rearranging and, in some cases, looking for furniture, hunting for lost writing implements, arguments over who was sitting next to whom, would continue well into the lesson. Whilst the Foundation Course itself incorporated its own aims and objectives, clearly our own teaching and survival objectives were to be far more fundamental in the early development of the course. Issues such as entry into the classroom; seating arrangements; individual possession of writing implements; organisation and presentation of written work; appropriate oral responses in discussion work; responsibility for learning; and consideration for others–all these factors and many more had to be addressed before tackling the syllabus realistically and effectively.

Our initial problem was that of unsuitable room arrangements which were not conducive to the well-ordered environment we sought. It was with considerable reluctance that we eventually took up residence in the suite of rooms which contained the Special Resource Department.

This option had always been open to us but in stressing the importance of the Foundation Course's being seen as a mainstream initiative, we had been anxious to site our base within the main school. In the event, the youngsters were as fed up as we were with our room-hopping activities and looked forward with anticipation to having a room of their own for 'C&G'– as the course had by then become known.

The suite itself comprised a carpeted central reception area with three small teaching rooms, a craft room, a fully-equipped kitchen and an office. Whilst the accommodation was originally provided to house thirty-five children at any one time, the increase in classroom support work for youngsters with special needs left the department vacated for much of the day, serving only very small groups of individuals for short periods. The suite was in fact a superb resource providing us with the craft room as our main base, the central area for practical group work, discussions and television/video presentations, the small teaching rooms, reception area and kitchen as spillover rooms for youngsters wishing to work in small groups or individually, and the office for counselling activities and, on some occasions 'individual study'. Additionally the department's adequate resources–TV, video, audio-visual camera, typewriters, overhead projectors, sinks, kettle, cooker and quite often unsuspecting staff–were utilised to the full.

The frequent presence of the SRD auxiliary staff within the teaching area proved to be of incalculable benefit to the youngsters who were often observed arriving early for lessons in the knowledge that a friendly welcome awaited them. Both members of the auxiliary staff were parents with youngsters who attended the school. There genuine interest and ability to 'listen' provided the youngsters with adults other than 'teachers' with whom they could identify and receive support.

Collaborative teaching

The advantage of working in a collaborative teaching situation during this period in particular was immensely beneficial. Classroom management skills were essential. The lesson would proceed, one of us taking responsibility for delivery, the other as inconspicuously as possible, pre-empting difficulties around the room, ensuring everyone possessed required materials and thus eliminating minor distractions which can interrupt the smooth flow of a lesson. Throughout we would either reverse our prescribed roles or work a kind of duet, each of us 'chipping in' as appropriate. Without exception the youngsters in this group lacked confidence in their own ability to succeed in ILEA's four aspects of achievement and so it was important that, once the lesson was underway, we would both move about the room offering individual help and encouragement and modifying teaching objectives to suit individual needs where necessary. In this way we were able to ensure that each youngster received a degree of individual attention and experienced some form of positive feedback during the lesson, thus enabling the youngsters to experience the sense of satisfaction and achievement that comes from being involved.

The support we were able to afford each other in this situation helped to forge the foundations for the positive development of the group as a whole. If we were to encourage co-operative group learning then it was important for us to be seen to be co-operating with one another in a democratic and caring way. Having shared together the planning of the lessons beforehand, it was sometimes necessary to modify our procedure during the course of the lesson according to the perceived need of the moment.

New ideas we would openly offer for consideration, initially between ourselves but subsequently including the youngster's opinions in the decisions which were reached. In this way the youngsters were able to observe two adults interacting naturally in agreement, in disagreement, in fun and often in confusion!

By including the students in our deliberations, the foundations were being laid for them to begin to take responsibility for their own learning within the group. The team-teaching approach produced positive benefits in terms of our management of both the group, of individual youngsters and our own professional development.

- Whilst one of us concentrated on the delivery, the other was able to observe the behaviour and reactions of individuals within the group more closely and in this way we were able to ascertain the effectiveness of our approach and make modifications accordingly.
- On occasions when one of us had been involved in confrontation with a youngster, it was possible for the first person to withdraw from the situation knowing that the other would follow through, thus helping to aviod unnecessary antagonism between the two parties whilst still reinforcing the teaching point.
- We were able to share each other's strengths and weaknesses, both teaching knowledge and skills, and learn from these.

- The mere presence of another adult in the room provided an often welcome outlet for the relief of tensions which might otherwise remain internalised and impair our performance both within the group and as individuals.

Group work

A very strong group identity already existed in that almost without exception these youngsters felt themselves to be 'failures' within the school environment. Several responded by playing truant, some through anti-social behaviour, some withdrawing into the passive state of total disinterest and all suffering from depressed self-esteem. Most felt bitter and articulated a strong sense of injustice.

Ironically it was upon this common group sense of failure that we built the foundations of success. From the premise that we were 'all in this together', that we all experienced difficulties at some time or another and that by being honest with each other and working together we would have a better chance of success, the group began to develop.

For example, at the onset of the course we outlined our proposals for the presentation of written work, which was to be on A4 paper, clearly headed with name, date and title underlined. This work was to be collated in a hard-backed file, the contents of which were to be continually updated in the index at the front. In the event, every youngster in the group found these tasks, identifiable in the first of ILEA's achievement aspects, difficult to negotiate. We spent considerable time taking the youngsters through this organisational procedure step by step, page by page. Some were experiencing general organisational difficulties: getting the punched holes on the left side, the paper the correct way up, using a ruler; others experienced difficulties in reading and writing their own work. We encouraged them to help each other in this task and by not rushing ahead with the next item until everyone was organised they began to share difficulties with their group study skills in a less self-conscious way. The start of each session always included an introduction to the new topic together with an outline of work to be completed from previous sessions. Some sessions were inevitably given over completely to 'catching up'. On these occasions youngsters would be actively working on a variety of tasks at different levels, those who had completed the set work more quickly being given the opportunity to research further into their particular area of interest. In this way youngsters were able to work at their own pace in the knowledge that they would not be 'left behind'. We ensured that everyone was given the same opportunity to achieve the learning objectives of the course, the indexing procedure helping them to record and monitor their work and progress.

Other members of staff, who came into contact with the group in the event of our absence, expressed amazement at the youngsters' ability to organise their own learning activities. It was reported back by members of the auxiliary staff that one teacher who had found himself 'covering' in my absence had actually sat in the adjoining office for the duration of a double period, apparently oblivious to the activities of the group in the teaching room. Whilst one cannot condone this irresponsible behaviour, it is clear that the framework supporting the procedure helped to provide a learning environment which became self-directive, an established routine which at times made the teaching staff superfluous. On occasions it was not also unusual to find ourselves almost redundant, a sharp contrast to our management procedures in the early weeks of the course!

The positive feelings of achievement experienced by the youngsters when they saw their work mounting into thick, well-organised files were well articulated, 'I've never written so much in my life', 'My Dad will never believe this, can we take our files home?' We capitalised on this new-found confidence by ensuring that the wall displays included current pieces of work from each member, written and pictoral. In this way the youngsters were encouraged to discuss and evaluate each other's work in an informal way which helped to reinforce positive feelings of achievement.

It was interesting as well as gratifying to observe the youngsters' responses and occasional disbelief, when we encouraged discussions about issues which were meaningful to them. Working within the themes of the Individual, the Individual and the Family, School and Friends, the Individual and the Law, the Individual and Society, we explored areas of interaction which dealt with the essentially individual business of being 'human'.

As it is commonly believed that our personal growth and development is achieved mainly through the part we play in the lives of others and they in ours, group work provided us with the ideal process through which to begin to encourage the youngsters to relate to each other and to take responsibility for their behaviour. In this way the moral, social and political influences developed from their own experiences and subsequently widened through the reflection of learning provided by the shared group experience.

At the beginning of a typical session, Richard was inevitably one of the last to 'settle' into the classroom, often requiring assistance to find a seat and organise his books. His inability to perform such menial tasks and the slowness of his verbal responses often caused considerable jeering and hilarity amongst his peers. John reluctantly appeared in the doorway, never coming inside of his own accord but always requiring polite invitation from us. His personal belongings slung together in a haphazard heap of screwed-up coverless books, interpersed with tatty pieces of paper, crisp packets and socks, were ritually tipped on to the desk at the start of each session–silently defying us to comment as he defined his boundaries. Peter's incessant voice in the background arguing vehemently that he didn't need qualifications anyway, he already had a job lined up with his Dad, so this was all just a waste of time when he could be out earning £200 a week. Susan excitedly recounting last evening's happenings to an admiring audience of somewhat less experienced friends; Jane bored as usual, impatiently waiting for proceedings to begin. James's predictable late arrival causing the inevitable disruption.

Much of our early work was spent in encouraging the group to focus on their own behaviour and how it affected both themselves and the others in the group. In order to have an understanding of another person there must be an appreciation of differences and such an appreciation was not evident, particularly in the group's response to Richard.

When we asked them why they found it necessary to laugh and make fun of him, they said that they felt he 'was lazy and acted daft to get out of things'. By asking Richard to respond to their accusations the group found themselves exploring and identifying with the kinds of difficulties Richard faced in attempting to cope with epilepsy, particularly his feelings of isolation and lack of self-confidence. During this session he also admitted with a wry smile that he was lazy and he did sometimes try to get out of things, but then don't we all?

One requirement of the course was that youngsters should show evidence of individual study. As an illustration of how they might approach this aspect of the course, we tentatively suggested that Richard might like to share his interest in astronomy with us. Not knowing quite what to expect, we were amazed to observe Richard struggling into school on the agreed day, dragging along two large suitcases bulging with his personal treasures. His enthusiasm was such that he totally captivated his surprised audience, describing with articulate fluency the meaning of astronomy, illustrating his talk with models, pictures, books and immaculately presented scrapbooks bulging with writing and illustrations. Such was the group interest that even John, who had refused to take his seat with the rest and was occupying himself in another room, was observed leaning round the door post and eventually taking up his seat with the others.

Not only did Richard's talk improve his standing within the group who subsequently began to take it in turns to help him with his classwork, it also increased the group's motivation to study for themselves in a similar way and stimulated suggestions for helping each other. One boy, Paul, who we suspected had never handed in a piece of homework in his life, on entry into the class one morning exclaimed, 'I did some topic work last night Miss', and with an expression of absolute incredulity continued, 'I don't know why ... but I did.' Another boy came up with the idea that if they made a list of their individual study topics to be displayed on the wall, they could all look out for material for each other, books, magazine cuttings and so on.

John, however, remained adamant that he did not need anyone's help and refused to have his name on the list. In the same way he was unable to conform to any activity in the learning situation. He always did things his own way. He refused, for example, to present readable written work, arguing that he couldn't write neatly. He knew what he was saying, so that was good enough for him. He didn't see the point in writing it down anyway.

The group themselves had been actively involved in the establishment of classroom rules, standards and procedures and this process of accountability encouraged them to consider alternative strategies for John to adopt. In consideration of John's feelings the group finally suggested that he might find it helpful to use a typewriter. By acknowledging John's problem and offering a positive solution to his difficulty, real or perceived, the group were able to assist John in reviewing his learning style and, by removing one of his barriers to learning, renewed his motivation to succeed. The group's approval of this arrangement was important to John as it acknowledged and accepted his need for individualism.

The group helped Peter in a number of ways. Initially they were quietly intrigued to know how we were going to respond to Peter's anti-school behaviour, some having an unspoken admiration for his outspoken confrontations with 'authority'. As the group developed and their trust in us grew their response to him became less supportive. They, as did we, ignored his aggressive outbursts and dismissed his attempts at collusion.

During a session covering the Individual and School, youngsters were given the opportunity to discuss, 'What makes a good teacher?' and 'What makes a bad teacher?' On many occasions Peter expressed his dissatisfaction for the way in which teachers treated him and his contribution to these sessions was illuminating. Within the context of classroom meetings the group assisted Peter to become more aware of his own behaviour, initially through an expressed concern that his negative approach to the course was hindering everyone else's chances of success and subsequently by sharing their own experiences of 'good' and 'bad' teachers in a way which evaluated the causes and effects of particular responses as they saw them.

Within the safe environment of his own peer group Peter was able to articulate his feelings freely. These were reflected back to him in a non-threatening but confronting way. It was Susan, for example, who deduced, 'You can't expect teachers to listen to you if you won't listen to them!' In this way Peter was assisted over a period of time to manage his interpersonal relationships in a more positive way, his successes and failures often being monitored by his classmates who observed his behaviour around school with a critical yet sympathetic eye.

Links with the community

We attempted to consolidate the group experience when we arranged an open day and encouraged the group to invite parents, friends, relatives, brothers and sisters to share in a day's activities. We took the opportunity of inviting teaching staff from both our own school (including caretakers and secretary) and others within the local community, the educational psychologist, adviser, educational welfare officer and any other agency representatives whom we knew to be involved with the youngsters, including social workers and employers. We invited representatives from the local college of further education with whom we had been working to develop closer curriculum liaison, PGCE students and teachers studying for a diploma course at the polytechnic. The day was structured so that the youngsters were actively involved in a variety of practical situations, some greeting and escorting visitors, some working with computers and audio-visual resources. Others were painting and cooking, providing constant hot mince pies and coffee for visitors who called in and out throughout the day.

All the youngsters were briefed to make the visitors feel both welcome and involved by explaining what they were doing and why. This they achieved with remarkable pride and panache. Such was the success generated and interest expressed that several of the 99 per cent turnout from parents returned for a second visit, bringing grandparents and neighbours for another look!

The positive feedback we received from parents was gratifying. Some of them had never been to the school before. Many of those who had had previously experienced negative feedback. Most expressed genuine amazement at their youngster's achievements. Several commented upon how they felt the children's attitude to school had changed and how often they spoke about what they had been doing in school these days.

The commitment of the youngsters themselves to the course was well illustrated by Steven, who only attended school on 'C&G' days and actually sent messages via friends for work to catch up with should he miss some, and James who always arrived sooner or later, and on the occasion of the open day, having been suspended from school during that week, cheerfully appeared through the back entrance. More sadly for John, who was found at the end of the day quietly fighting back his tears of disappointment, his Mum never arrived, the rest of the group offering consolation he refused to accept.

The objectives of the Foundation Course were related as closely as possible to the youngster's local community and treated in a practical way thereby making the most of available opportunities for visits to local caring institutions, visiting speakers and community/work experience. In planning a residential experience where we would be doing conservation work for the National Trust we linked up with a group of PGCE students from the polytechnic.

The opportunity was taken to spend a day visiting the institution. The youngsters were shown around the students' halls of residence, refectory, social and sports facilities. They were introduced to the library by the college librarian who showed them how to use the library effectively through the use of basic retrieval skills, the Dewey system of classification and the microfiche. The PGCE students assisted the youngsters in trying out the different systems. They were given a 'hands-on' computer experience in the Educational Methods Unit and a practical introduction to the Audio-Visual Centre.

Prior to the visit, the group themselves had to make several difficult decisions. This particular trip had been the outcome of our anticipated National Trust Conservation Week in Devon. Whilst this residential experience was an integral part of the Foundation Course, it was not obligatory, and two group members could not be persuaded to join the week's activity, in spite of considerable discussion within the group and 'gentle persuasion' from us.

When the trip to the polytechnic was announced, the issue was raised by some of the youngsters, that if the two in question did not wish to participate in the residential experience, they did not have the right to visit the polytechnic. The two in question, both being computer fanatics, did not wish to be left out of this experience.

My own feeling which I expressed to the group, was that as the two individuals could not give constructive reasons as to why they did not wish to join us in Devon, other than 'I don't want to come', they would have to sacrifice the extra benefits which were a natural outcome of the trip. I was over-ruled on this occasion.

In addition, the point was raised that Peter's recent disruptive behaviour seemed to indicate that he might not be able to conduct himself in a responsible way. After considerable discussion the group decided that he must be given the benefit of the doubt and should also be allowed to go. They reasoned that if he could not behave himself on a day trip, perhaps he could not be trusted on a week's visit.

In the event Peter's subsequent behaviour on this visit was totally unacceptable. He was deliberately and unnecessarily rude to the PGCE students, dismissing their overtures of friendship with verbal abuse and by totally dismissive behaviour, on one occasion turning his back and walking away. This was an example of one of those 'crisis' situations in which the presence of two adults enabled us to make an immediate response. Whilst one of us remained to monitor the group activity, the other was able to withdraw Peter from the situation, containing and counselling him in total isolation for as long as was necessary.

Peter accepted that his behaviour was unacceptable but justified his response by claiming that he was always bad tempered if he did not have a cigarette in the mornings. Our early morning departure from school apparently had deprived him of this opportunity.

Having stressed to Peter that his justification for his behaviour was not acceptable on this occasion, he was left outside the television studio in which the group were working, the door slightly ajar. His own inquisitiveness to see the film of his peers being transmitted on the screen, coupled with our own anxiety that he should not be unsupervised, resulted in his eventual presence at the back of the room. At this point, the lecturer conducting the session, being unaware of Peter's position of disgrace, actually drew him into conversation and ultimately back within the group.

Our final venue of the day was spent relaxing in the adult atmosphere of the Students Union Bar and it was here that Peter was faced with the reality of his actions. His peers, having witnessed his behaviour and having no sympathy for his condition, felt that he had 'let them down', particularly as it was they who had insisted that he must be given the chance to 'prove' himself on this outing. They could be heard as they sat huddled on bar stools, telling him that they thought he was being stupid and showing off, that they couldn't see what he had to be so rude about when everyone there was being so good to them, giving up their time when they didn't have to. Peter told them that he was bored in the library. Susan replied that she thought he just used 'boredom' as an excuse to please himself, Jane intervened with the comment, 'Well so was I, but that doesn't mean to say I can swear at people ... the computers made up for it anyway!'

This additional group pressure assisted Peter to accept responsibility for his inappropriate behaviour and encouraged him to offer his apologies at the time. Later he was able to consider ways in which he could overcome his apparent problem with the help of the group who, led by Susan, remained anxious to help him out. Within the classroom setting the next day, some time was spent considering how Peter's perceived problem might affect us all should we allow him to join us on our week away. Were we, for example, to be expected to tolerate similar abuse from Peter, just because he had not smoked his early-morning cigarette? Was it fair of him to expect us to do so?

It was therefore a natural outcome of the group's experience that we should find ourselves considering the whole issue of drug dependency, cigarette smoking, alcholism, glue sniffing; the causes and effects on addicts, their families and friends. Interestingly, during the course of the week away, smoking was not an issue of any concern, although Peter could be observed most mornings, taking my dog for an early morning stroll before the day's activities began.

Counselling and the recording of achievement

The essence of counselling is good listening and the reflection of feelings which will encourage individuals to grow, to move forward. These were qualities which we encouraged from the youngsters themselves whilst also offering them individual counselling from ourselves. The presence of two adults gave us the added advantage of having more time to devote to individuals in the classroom setting (an advantage which was commented upon by the youngsters themselves who appreciated the extra attention we were able to afford) as well as enabling us to offer more immediate 'crisis' counselling and one-to-one interviews twice a term.

We devised a profile system which was used in conjunction with a half-termly assessment sheet. The assessment sheet completed by ourselves covered oral, written, group, project, illustrative and general progress reports together with two overall grades for effort and achievement. The youngsters were asked to fill in an assessment profile which asked them to consider issues such as which parts of the course they had most/least enjoyed, found most difficult, most useful and so on. In addition they were asked to identify areas in which they felt they could improve upon with a little more effort, as well as indicating areas for study not already included in the course. Finally they were asked to identify three goals which they felt they needed to aim for during the next term.

Having completed our respective sheets, we arranged individual interviews with the youngsters and we were able to discuss and analyse our/their progress so far, using the information contained in the sheets as a starting point. In this way we were able to consider the positive aspects as we saw them, offering the appropriate verbal encouragement as well as exploring the negative aspects and looking at ways of improving them. The youngsters themselves were able to respond in a positive way because they had come to understand that their views would be considered: they had a 'stake' in their own learning and mutual respect had began to evolve. The interview culminated in a negotiated contract of agreed areas for improvement during the next half term, at the end of which we would review the situation again.

The increased motivation achieved through the feeling of involvement in this formative process was illustrated when four of the youngsters, two boys and two girls, having independently negotiated their attendance with the member of staff in charge, 'self-referred' themselves to a handwriting class within the Special Resource Department.

The residential community work experience

The National Trust offer cheap, well-equipped and comfortable accommodation in return for several days' conservation work which provided us with a residential experience designed to complement a term's work in environmental and social studies. The trip afforded the youngsters the opportunity to try out their new-found skills of co-operative and purposeful planning, together with the opportunity to relate positively to a group of previously unknown individuals within a different setting.

The financial and material resources at our disposal were enhanced by our links with the polytechnic. Not only did it provide us with an extra vehicle for transportation and reimburse the fuel costs, it also provided us with twelve 22-year-old PGCE students who joined us as part of their practical training course.

The youngsters themselves were involved in the practical planning, costing and organisation of the trip. They chose the menus, taking into account individual preferences as far as was practicable and gave particular attention to providing well-balanced yet quickly prepared meals. Together with a member of staff, half of the group visited the local cash and carry to purchase their provisions where they were also faced with the added complications of 'buying in bulk'! The other half of the group were occupied working out cooking and cleaning rotas. It was interesting to witness their deliberations in deciding who would best work together. For example, knowing that James always overslept in the mornings, Susan suggested that she might work with him, because she always woke early and could 'get him up'. Whenever Richard's name appeared on the rota, they made sure that one person was given specific responsibility for helping him, eventually deciding that this person would be an 'extra' member of the team who was there just to make sure that he did his bit! They included in these rotas both the staff and the students.

The week's programme involved two full days' conservation work which was to prove as much of a challenge for the staff and students as it was for the youngsters. The work involved planting four hundred trees across a wide area of generally inhospitable terrain. On the first day and led by the warden we were given an impressive demonstration of how the task was to be achieved. Everyone was feeling slightly overwhelmed by the apparent enormity of our task but none more so than Richard who, having realised the implications of the situation before us, refused to watch the warden's demonstration turning his back with grim determination.

The work was physically hard and demanded considerable perseverance. The experience of small working-group isolation afforded everyone the opportunity to begin to get to know each other and surprisingly the youngsters adapted to the situation resonably quickly, unlike the students who had not bargained for anything quite like this. The youngsters not happy, but anxious to prove themselves to the students, the students torn between their professional role of trainee teachers and their preferred role of carefree students who could not quite reconcile the fact that coffee would not be served at half-hour intervals.

Only gradually came the realisation that the task in hand could not be avoided and the groups began to settle into a co-operative working routine, one clearing, one digging, one planting. As so often happens when individuals are engaged in a common activity, it was not long before the element of competition was introduced with groups vying with each other to plant the most trees. During lunch, strategies for the most efficient deployment of manpower were heatedly discussed and argued.

The residential setting provided the youngsters with the opportunity to find their own 'level', to make their own decisions and to be themselves which in turn provided the opportunity for staff to observe developmental needs which had not revealed themselves in the school environment but which could be effectively responded to on our return.

For Richard this was a unique experience, never having been away without his family before. Clearly during the early part of the week Richard missed his mother. On these occasions he became tearful and made the unrealistic demand 'I want my Mum, I want to see her now,' displaying the childlike temper tantrums of a five year old. David, a particularly sensitive 14 year old who anxiously avoided any kind of group activity in school and who was also away from home for the first time, brought with him his teddy bear. Jane, having formed a close attachment to a student in her working party on the first day, became totally transformed, self-assured, cheerful and friendly. James revealed the personal qualities which obviously made him so popular with his peers. He was a natural comic, keeping everyone amused with his light-hearted humour as he 'waited on' at meal times. He was always in the right place at the right time and could be relied upon to plan and carry out tasks of responsibility and displayed considerable leadership qualities. Whether through fear of rejection by his peers, or the anxiety of facing the students to whom he had previously been so rude, Peter appeared genuinely relaxed in this environment. His conversation and behaviour revealed a previously undisclosed maturity which none of us would have believed possible. One member of the teaching staff commented that he would not have believed it if he had not seen it for himself.

In the more relaxed evening atmosphere the youngsters and students shared experiences and personal confidences which helped to strengthen feelings of involvement and commitment to the group activity. This whole-group experience formed the perfect vehicle through which new relationships could be formed and a new group identity emerge. From this point the group began to organise their own activities. The students planned games in which it was encouraging to observe both David and Richard enthusiastically taking active parts in group games which they had hitherto found so threatening. In return the youngsters planned, rehearsed and performed their own review involving everyone but led by James and starring Richard complete with glitter make-up, who introduced the acts. It was encouraging also to observe Jill remove the scarf which she both lived and slept in and which caused so much unnecessary controversy at school.

A penultimate comment from one youngster, made during a brief lull in the musical entertainments we provided each other on our return journey was, 'I thought Peter was going to be awful, a real pain, but you weren't were you Peter? You were great.' The flush of pride which appeared on Peter's face said it all. A student commented 'I am impressed at the level of maturity the group have displayed, at the beginning of the week they seemed so childish.'

Lessons had been learned by us all.

Resources for use in the pastoral curriculum: meeting developmental and special needs

The purpose of this chapter is to introduce and briefly describe a selection of resources which have been effectively used in the pastoral curriculum.

There is a vast range of resources available for use in the 14–18 pastoral curriculum. It is easy to be seduced by attractively produced packages and materials, particularly if they have been extensively advertised. The availability of so much material places constraints upon effective selection. The questions the teacher consistently has to ask are:

Is this resource adaptable to the situation in which it is going to be used?
Is it an effective resource which will help me meet some of the perceived needs of youngsters in the group?
Do I feel at ease using this resource?
Will this resource complement my personal resources?

The selection of resources, the tools of the trade, generally comes down to personal choice. The following resources are those which have been observed being effectively used in schools, units and colleges. It is a selective and by no means exclusive list and is merely indicative of some of the resources available. Resources for staff development are described in the final chapter.

BOOKS AND PROJECTS

Ashbee, C. (ed.)   (1984)   *Real Life Maths Skills*
(Heinemann Educational)
Divided into units which include opportunities for experiential and problem-solving learning.

Ball, M.   (1986)   *In Our Own Right: Beyond the Label of Physical Disability*
(CSV)
Challenges the concept of disability as a 'disabling' condition; emphasises the achievement possibilities for disabled people.

Barrett, R. and Green, G.   (1983)   *Day to Day English - Books 1 and 2*
(Longman)
These books are the results of the 'Hertfordshire English project', a basic English course linked to life-skills teaching.

Bleiman, B.   (1985)   *Assignments 16–19*
(Longman)
A resource for language and communication which can be used in CPVE and pre-vocational courses. It encourages the development of a wide range of skills: reading, writing, talking, listening, research, picture and study skills. It raises a number of pertinent issues, particularly those of unemployment and work experience.

Brandes, D. and Phillips, H.   (1979)   *Gamesters' Handbook*
(Hutchinson)
A comprehensive collection of trust games which can be effectively used in group work. They have to be used with sensitivity and their aims made explicit to the participants. I have observed people being threatened and anxious in learning situations where they have been used crudely. They are an excellent resource but their use can occasionally become distorted.

Canfield, J. and Welsh, H.   (1976)   *100 Ways to Enhance Self Concept in the Classroom*
(Prentice Hall)
The aim of this practical caring resource is to build a self-enhancing classroom climate. The book contains a range of activity-orientated classroom suggestions which encourage the development of a positive self concept. It is constructed around the themes of

- building an environment of positive support
- my strengths
- who am I?
- accepting my body
- where am I going?
- the language of self and
- relationships with others.

There is a comprehensive annotated bibliography.

Cheston, M. (1979) *It's Your Life*
(Religious and Moral Education Press–Arnold Wheaton)

A well-organised introductory text to personal and social educa-tion issues. Three parts: yourself, your surroundings, your relationships. Each issue takes up a double page which contains (i) a short introduction; (ii) a think and discuss section, with an occasional quiz; (iii) a work out/find out section; and finally (iv) a work for folders section. It is a book for dipping into: it effectively arouses interest about issues which can be developed further.

Culshaw, C. and Waters, D. (1984) *Headwork Books 1, 2, 3, and 4*
(Oxford University Press)

The books aim to help less able youngsters read with under-standing. A range of subjects are covered, each page containing a problem situation. Youngsters are encouraged to use a range of skills to solve the problem.

Culshaw, C. (1987) *Headwork Stories: Books 1 and 2*
(Oxford University Press)

These books which complement the preceding books, contain a range of stories which provoke discussion and speculation.

Flinn, J. (1985) *Working Work Out*
(Collins)

This is one of a number of books currently on offer which presents a package approach to skill training for work. It even has a profile form at the end. It is useful to dip into, and it can encourage further exploration of some of the issues raised. My only concern is that some staff will merely use a booklet like this as a superficial package to skill training.

Gann, N. (1975) *Tracy Congdon/Terry Parker*
(Community Service Volunteers)

Two stimulating simulation excercises which focus upon the problems people have to face when they have to make decisions based upon conflicting evidence. Each attractively produced pack contains:

- background sheets to the case under discussion (the back-ground sheet in the Tracy Congdon pack describes the participatory characters)
- the situation
- the brief

- additional help.

There is an accompanying role sheet which elaborates upon the characters and succinct teacher's notes accompany each pack. This is an excellent resource. CSV can supply a wide range of supportive resources for use in the process curriculum.

Gillespie, J. (1983, 2nd) *Numbers at Work*
(National Extension College)

A very attractively produced book. The emphasis is upon problem-solving and decision/making within adult situations, i.e. slimming, DIY, saving on heat. The material is directly relevant to current everyday living.

Green, K. *et al.* (1986) *The Ark Environmental Investigator's Kit*
(Community Unit, Central Independent TV)

A lively conservation project which covers a range of environmental issues. Demands quite a high level of conceptual awareness.

Health Education Project (1983) *Fit for Life*
(Schools Council/Health Education Council)

Level 2 (9–12 yrs) Level 3 (13+)

Health-education materials particularly useful for youngsters with learning difficulties. Topics raised are developmentally significant for adolescents even though they are produced for youngsters who may experience difficulty grasping abstract concepts. Each pack contains a detailed teacher's guide plus 94 worksheet photocopy masters for Level 2 and 116 for Level 3. Extensive resource lists are given at the end of each section. The materials have been extensively trialled in schools. Most attractive format and highly topical material makes them an exceptional resource pack for use in the classroom.

Hopson, B. and Hough, P. (1982) *Exercises in Personal and Career Development*
(CRAC)

Has a range of activity-based resource examples: questionnaires, role-play exercises, games and worksheets which promote self-assessment and decision-making.

Hopson, B. and Scully, M. (1980, 1982 and 1986) *Lifeskills Teaching Programmes 1, 2 and 3*
(Lifeskills Associates)

An excellent, comprehensive loose-leaf resource which emphasises personal skill development, e.g. time management, study skill questionnaire, distinct study skill acquisition, how to manage stress, how to find a job, how to cope with unemployment. An essential pack which contains worksheets for reproduction.

Jackson, D. (ed.) (1976) *Family and School*
(Ward Lock Educational)

An attractive collection of contemporary sources which develop the title theme. This book comes from the English Project: a series of anthologies which contains stimulating and imaginative choice of material. The project is organised in three stages and the books cover such themes as 'Things working', 'That once was me', 'Alone', 'Identity', 'Faces in the crowd'. Provocative material ideal for use in active group work.

Kaye-Besley, L. and Byles, D. (1984) *Skills for Life*
(Stanley Thorne)

An exploration of transitional skills for use in school and beyond. The three sections, 'Community Services', 'A Place in the Community', 'Becoming a Worker in the Community' are split into units. There is a heavy reliance upon information conveyance but through other activities it also attempts to encourage the young person to become actively involved in the learning process.

Laxton, B. and Rawlinson, G. (1977) *Make it Count*
(National Extension College)

Another attractively produced book from the NEC. It introduces the youngster to the basic processes of number for use within a problem-solving environment. The 'Bingo' activities, page 4, arouse intense initial interest in the activities. Youngsters need to be guided through the exercises.

Longman, K. (1981) *Learning for Life*
(Macmillan Educational)

A comprehensive text which is organised around six units: 'This is You', 'The Choice is Yours', 'Thinking about Work', 'Looking for Work', 'Starting Work' and 'Equal Opportunities'. A series of exercises accompany each unit, to be developed within guided group work sessions. The book emphasises the importance of the individual, and the need for problem-solving skills which will enable informed decisions to be made.

Mayblin, B. and Shaw, G.   (1984)   *No Bed No Job*
(CSV)
Board game which explores problems of unemployment and
homelessness amongst young people.

McPhail, P.,   (1972)   *Lifeline–Moral Education in the Secondary School*
(Longman)
This project, although very dated, is of considerable value in the
classroom. It emphasises problem-solving within a caring group
environment. The aim is to 'develop the ability to predict
possible, and probable consequences if we are to behave morally'
(McPhail, 1972). The material gradually moves the adolescent
away from concrete one-to-one situations to small-group relationships which demand more abstract and complex thought.

The material is arranged in four groups: (a) *'In other people's shoes'*;
comprising three sets of cards which present situations as starting
points; (b) *'Proving the rule'* five short booklets which centre on the
character of Paul and his relations with family, friends and
society; (c) *'What would you have done?'* six booklets which consider
moral and social problems based upon incidents from the recent
past; and (d) *'Our school'* a handbook for encouraging democracy
within the school. The development of process starts with

- the individual and his relationships in a one-to-one situation
- in small groups
- in the wider society and
- the cyclical process brings the practicalities of decision-making back to the individual within his own school.

Meredith, S.   (1985)   *Growing Up*
(Usborne Publishing)
Explains the processes of change during puberty in a straightfor-
ward and explicit way. It has an attractive presentation, cartoons
and drawings. The book refers to issues of concern for youngsters
which are not often dealt with, e.g., feeling gangly, shaving,
breast size, buying a bra, myths about periods, penis size, wet
dreams, being too fat. Contains useful glossary and further
resources section. The equally useful accompanying volume
'Babies', is produced in the Usborne 'Facts of Life' series.

Merseyside and Cheshire Numeracy
Lift Off Project   (1985)   *Begin Here Numbers Start Here*
(Adult Literacy and Basic Skills Unit)
Two packs of highly stimulating and valuable material. Resources include wall charts, problem-solving games and worksheets which encourage active group work and a problem-solving approach to maths. Materials are adaptable to a wide variety of situations.

Mills, J., Mills, R. and Stringer, L.   (1985)   *Choices*
(Oxford University Press)
The book is attractive in presentation and provides material which encourages the development of oral, reading, and writing skills. Organised around four themes–viewpoints, time off, challenges, and study skills. Concludes with a skills' checklist.

Minett, P.   (1985)   *Child Care and Development*
(John Murray)
A factual, comprehensive and readable text, accompanied by photographs, cartoons and diagrams. Organised in 64 self-contained topics within 8 sections. Each topic contains information, questions, extended activity and an interesting section called 'Child Study' which encourages youngsters to observe children actively as they develop. Each section contains a selection of pertinent exercises.

Morrison, C.   (1982)   *Skills for Living*
(Macdonald Educational)
A six-part series for underachievers which covers a range of skills. Worksheets contain information and a variety of tasks. The six areas are: basic form filling; money (2); communicating; settling down; and getting about. There is an accompanying teacher's manual.

Wilson, F.   (1983)   *Ambush!*
(Careers Research Advisory Council)
A snakes and ladders game for five players where points are gained when job-search skills are effectively recognised. One of the many valuable resources produced by CRAC.

USEFUL ADDRESSES

Brook Advisory Centres,
153A East Street,
London SE17

Careers Education Resource Centre,
National Institute of Careers Education and Counselling,
Bayfordbury House,
Lower Hatfield Road,
Hertford SG13 8LD

Careers Research Advisory Council,
Hobsons Press (Cambridge) Limited,
Bateman Street,
Cambridge CB2 1LZ

City and Guilds of London Institute,
76 Portland Place,
London W1

Community Service Volunteers Advisory Service,
237 Pentonville Road,
London N1 9NJ

Department of Industry,
Ashdown House,
123 Victoria Street,
London SW1E 6RB

Equal Opportunities Commission,
Overseas House,
Quay Street,
Manchester M3 3HN

Further Education and Curriculum Review and Development Unit (FEU),
Publications Despatch Centre,
Honeypot Lane,
Canon's Park,
Stanmore,
Middlesex HA7 1AZ

Health Education Council,
78 New Oxford Street,
London WC1A 1AM

Health Education Resources Centre,
71–75 New Oxford Street,
London WC1A 1AH

ILEA Careers Education Resource Centre,
377 Clapham Road,
London SW9 9BT

ILEA Learning Materials Service,
Publishing Centre,
Highbury Station Road,
London N1 1SB

Lifeskills Associates,
Ashling,
Back Church Lane,
Leeds LS16 8DN

Moral Education Resource Centre,
St Martin's College,
Lancaster LA1 3JD

National Extension College,
8 Brooklands Avenue,
Cambridge CB2 2HN

New Horizon,
1 Macklin Street,
London WC2
(Helps young people alone in London)

Outset,
30 Craven Street,
London WC2
(Mobilises volunteers to help those in need)

Relaxation for Living,
Dunesk, 29 Burwood Park Road,
Walton-on-Thames,
Surrey KT12 5LH

Schools Council Industry Project,
101 Great Portland Street,
London W1N 5FA

Schools Council Skills for Adult
  Working Life Project,
101 Great Portland Street,
London W1N 5FA

Teachers' Advisory Council on
  Alcohol and Drug Education,
2 Mount Street,
Manchester M2 5NG

The Family Planning Association
  Education Unit,
27–35 Mortimer Street,
London W1N 7RJ

The National Audio-Visual Aids
  Centre and Library,
Paxton Place,
Gipsy Road,
London SE27 9SR

The Samaritans,
17 Uxbridge Road,
Slough,
Bucks SL1 1SN

Understanding British Industry Re-
  source Centre,
Sun Alliance House,
New Inn Hall Street,
Oxford OX1 2QE

Part Four Special needs and staff development

Curriculum innovation will underfunction if it is not accompanied by a well-structured caring staff development programme. If pastoral care is to be an integrative curriculum influence, then it should simultaneously involve care staff as well as youngsters.

The processes which underpin staff development should reflect those pastoral processes which have been the subject of this book. Staff-development activities which relate to and extend issues raised in preceding chapters are given. This part concludes with a description of useful resources which can support INSET processes within schools which profess whole-school approaches to special education.

Change and staff needs

The purpose of this chapter is to consider the process of staff development as an integral aspect of pastoral care within the curriculum.

It is increasingly recognised that a number of young people leave school poorly equipped to cope with the demands of life beyond school. The plethora of current initiatives is in part a response to this situation. The centralised projection of these initiatives is packaged, presentable and in some instances reasonably palatable for the busy teacher and administrator to swallow. There is however within the profession anxiety and an increasingly low morale during a period of radical change within secondary education.

A disturbing development within secondary education is the increasing stratification of youngsters. The DES appears to retain responsibility for the academic curriculum, i.e. GCSE, AS levels, A levels and CPVE. The MSC will focus upon vocationally orientated studies, i.e. TVEI plus the two-year YTS with a remedial education component for potentially unemployable youngsters. This grouping of youngsters is far more insidious than the old school categories of secondary modern, grammar and technical.

Although youngsters then were rigorously categorised they could hold on to the empowering knowledge that they could obtain work. Take this away and a youngster retains a total dependency upon centralised curriculum directives. Chapter 3, however, illustrated how the core processes of a number of these initiatives can perform an integrative curriculum function. This whole-school approach has far-reaching implications for the ways in which schools are managed and the curriculum is designed, developed and evaluated: 'If the responsibility for meeting all educational needs in a local community is to remain where it belongs, with all of us–there are pressures that have to be diverted and converted into joint response' (Sayer, 1987).

This joint response involves a freeing of both management and curricular boundaries. The proverbial new patch of cloth sewn onto an old coat illustrates the strains and stresses which are imposed in a school which merely tinkers with curriculum change. The old curriculum coat has been wearing thin for years. There has been a consistent criticism that its system of delivery has failed numerous youngsters. Its warps and wefts–represented through class teaching, arbitary grouping of youngsters, inappropriate teaching materials, sterile learning processes and iniquitous forms of assessment–have lost credibility. To graft on a new patch, be it the flexible grouping of youngsters, developmental group work, formative methods of assessment, will only in the long term wear the coat even thinner.

A radical change in the ways in which we both manage and develop our secondary curricula does not mean overnight revolution, but it does mean an acknowledgement that education is developmental and evolutionary in nature.

EXAMPLES OF 14–18 INNOVATION

National Association of Head Teachers

One initiative which is worthy of note and which appears to make a radical visionary response to the 14–18 curriculum is that proposed by the NAHT. The kernel of the proposals is contained in this statement:

> But above all we are asking if the proposals in this document will establish new routes for young people to follow that fuse the vocational with the non-vocational, will remove institutional barriers so that the learning process along the chosen route can occur in an appropriate combination of school, college, training workplace or adult education centre, and will allow the degree of flexibility needed to bring about a high extension of opportunity

(NAHT, January 1986)

The paper takes up some of the issues previously raised when it refers to the 'expressed needs of society' which 'are a mass of contradictions'. Instead the proposals ignore the tendency to graft innovatory components on to an existing model. In an attempt to rationalise the education and training needs of young people, it is proposed that there should be a continuum of modular curriculum provision for 14–18 year olds.

Through a modular system, underpinned by an essential programme of tutorial work, young people would be able to follow a negotiated, integrated curriculum organised broadly around four areas which reflect both Hargreaves (1984) and Erikson's (1968) areas of concern:

(i)   academic
(ii) practical
(iii) technical
(iv) vocational.

Of importance is the recognition that all youngsters of whatever ability need the opportunity to succeed in as wide an area of learning as possible.

There would be Boards of Activity which would co-ordinate educational and training activity between institutions on a local level, and youngsters would have the opportunity to transfer between routes of experience in different institutional settings as necessary.

Assessment would be based upon a formative process of criteria assessment and it would contain a wide overview of a student's successes and experiences at different stages of his/her career. There should be financial support paid to the family up to the age of 16. After that age a student should be paid a common personal allowance. Such a scheme would then assist in eradicating some of the financial anomalies currently present within the system.

Inner London Education Authority

Equally radical curricular proposals are contained in the Hargreaves Report (1984). These develop from a belief in a modular system of curriculum organisation.

A simplistic definition of a module is that it is a component of learning which can either stand on its own, or one which develops linearity with other modules. A module can be fitted into a block of modules which form a tailor-made programme for the individual student. Hargreaves expounds upon the rationale which lies behind a modular approach to learning. In so doing he succinctly summarises the underlying tenets of the process curriculum.

> A half-term Unit permits a form of pupil involvement which is very difficult to achieve in a 2 year course. The syllabus content is relatively small, so the pupils can see clearly the knowledge and skills they need to acquire over the next few weeks. Course objectives, instead of existing only in the teacher's mind or the course design, can now be shared with the pupils. If pupils see clearly where they are going, they are more likely to be motivated to make the journey. Once unit objectives have been shared between teacher and pupil it is easier for teacher and pupil to negotiate the *means* by which unit goals can be reached. In other words, there can be joint planning of methods and procedures of work. This takes pupils out of passive roles into active and collaborative roles with the teacher. At the end of the unit, teachers and pupils can overtly and jointly evaluate the extent to which unit

objectives have been achieved. This helps to motivate pupils for the beginning of the next unit. It also makes it genuinely possible for the pupils to play an active role in curriculum development and evaluation.

At the end of each unit all pupils can be offered a clear and tangible assessment, each unit must give the pupil 'Something to show' for the six to eight weeks work ... Whatever the format of the unit credit, its existence will, we believe, enhance pupil motivation for the unit as well as for the succeeding units, since the units are cumulative. Moreover the unit credit is a permanent record of achievement (and the quality of the credit format should reflect this) so that even if a pupil does not ultimately enter for public examination the credit remains

(Hargreaves, 1984)

The modules would be organised in half-term units in years four and five and youngsters encouraged to choose modules based upon six compulsory broad elements which would take up 25 periods in a 40-period week. The remaining 15 periods would allow free options to be chosen or deeper concentration upon further study within the compulsory elements.

Staff development issues

Teachers within schools have to make a collective response to curriculum innovation. The quality of this response depends to a large extent upon the state of preparedness of the teaching profession to meet the demands of curriculum design, development and evaluation and in so doing influence the crucial ends and means of the educative process.

Curriculum innovation currently has a low priority for those headteachers who are coping with the day-to-day maintenance pressures of running a comprehensive school. Curriculum initiatives and packages for the 14–19 age group are a burgeoning market. Introduce them into a school, which has little time to evaluate their relevance for the particular school situation, and they eventually become swallowed, undigested and rarely assimilated into the school system.

Curriculum innovation, particularly in some secondary schools, is theorised on an abstract level which has little meaning for some teachers who are grappling with the day-to-day meaning of being there, in the classroom. A large number of secondary-school teachers are notorious isolationists, there is an intuitiveness about their teaching which often goes on behind closed doors. They might be superb teachers, but the skills and awareness somehow cannot be shared. Hargreaves observes, 'Teachers are short of feedback

... they have little time to take stock'. He further makes the point, 'Once teachers are deeply entrenched in their expert status and didactic style, the loss in the capacity to learn makes teachers afraid of learning' (Hargreaves, 1982).

Many teachers are afraid and some are anxious: of other colleagues, of disturbing pupils, of parents and of curriculum innovation. There is a particular kind of tiredness which comes about because many teachers are working at a maintenance, stop-gap level throughout the school day, including 'break'times.

For some the tiredness comes in part because they are going through the motions. They feel unchallenged, undervalued and under stress. It affects staff at all levels, yet somehow many do not feel 'safe' enough to articulate *their* needs particularly to colleagues, they just 'burn out' towards the weekends and holidays. At what cost to real curriculum innovation?

STAFF DEVELOPMENT PROCESSES

Positive staff development is a process whereby staff on an individual and a group basis can be helped to become effective and fulfilled on both a personal and professional level within the learning situation. Staff development within the area of the pastoral care of needs is little different from any other INSET (in-service educational-training) process.

Interestingly, Sayer challenges a view expressed by Fish (1985) that 'an important factor to bear in mind is that the amount of training should be related to the incidence and complexity of special educational needs'. Sayer rightly and logically offers the crucial observation that such a view does not 'touch the partnership of transaction'. If we really are involved in whole-school approaches to special education, then staff development is not about 'amounts of training'. It has to have as its focus the need to share skills and expertise across both management and curricular structures. We have to adjust to a view of education which sees all within the school as equal partners in the educative response to both developmental and special needs of all participants.

A developmental learning programme for staff should reflect those processes which youngsters should experience within a facilitative learning environment.

It is conjectured that any caring staff development programme should contain two interrelated strands:

- pre-facilitative
- awareness raising and realistic skill acquisition.

(1)   The pre-facilitative stage

This stage has close similarities to the pre-helping stage of counselling described in Chapter 6. It involves encouraging staff to feel psychologically secure with each other. They cannot experience this if they do not have the opportunity to work with each other, across departmental and management boundaries.

> At break times all staff in one school had coffee in their own departments. The constraints of both time and the site layout encouraged this. A concentrated effort was then made for coffee to be made available in the staffroom on two mornings per week. These two sessions became priority periods when staff from, for example, the maths and the humanities departments could actually talk with each other outside the constraints of department boundaries.

There is an urgent need, during the school working period for all staff to have the opportunity to come together to articulate needs, concerns, share expertise, skills, strengths and, more importantly, mutual reassurance. They need to 'tune' into each other: this is a key strand of any group-counselling environment. This means giving each other full attention, it means 'active' listening, it means reflecting back feelings and concerns. How many staffrooms encourage such a process?

A facilitative staffroom environment encourages staff to stand aside from role ascriptions whereby they feel 'safe' enough to talk about and share the good and bad feelings about being there, often in an isolated role, within the classroom.

(2)   Awareness-raising and skill acquisition

We all work from our own idelogical baselines. Through the process of participatory exploration, however, it is possible to reach concensus which takes into account individual differences and concerns. Staff need the opportunity to explore issues in depth. There is a recurring mismatch between the conceptual levels of staff, in part because they have not had the opportunity to explore as a group staff issues which affect the quality of teaching within the classroom.

Take, for example, assessment processes within the General Certificate of Secondary Education. Staff know that innovative procedures for assessment are an integral part of the initiative but ask what they understand by formative assessment and summative recording procedures and they, understandably, are somewhat non-plussed.

Awareness-raising involves analysing the situation in which

development is to take place. So often curriculum innovation fails because the prevailing situation, with its facilitative and restrictive influences, is ignored. This explorative exercise encourages staff to look at their own situation, to evaluate it critically, mindful of external influences and demands. They are then in a much more informed position to assess the validity of innovation for their curriculum, enabling it to be effectively incorporated into the fabric of the school.

Management issues

The management structure of any school has to reflect the curriculum emphasis of that environment. Paisey's assertion is that 'Management is about human activity', and 'managerial capacity in the teacher is less an optional extra which some teachers ought to have, more a necessary part of the professional qualification and achievement of every teacher' (Paisey, 1981).

If we are genuinely concerned that management should be about 'human activity' then it follows that all participants, youngsters and staff, are managers to different degrees within the school environment. The key issue is how do all personnel within the organisation manage management? Are we secure enough to come from behind our roles and share in the tasks of management and, in so doing, own responsibility for the equilibrium of the school?

Curriculum issues

A basic understanding is needed of the principles of curriculum design, development, implementation and evaluation. There has to be an additional awareness of the assumptions which often lie behind the 'officially' documented aims and objectives of the curriculum and, more importantly, behind the 'hidden curriculum', which is influenced by the ways in which we value the individual.

Human resources

An analysis is needed of the range of human resources which can be drawn upon to enhance the learning climate. We are poor models for youngsters. Very rarely do we openly co-operate and collabora-tively develop our teaching with colleagues, let alone with young people. Instead we are regularly seen by youngsters as adults who only co-operate when engaged in a form of apparent collusive activity designed to exert control over young people. How much more productive the learning process is when youngsters witness adults laughing together, sharing a problem, bringing youngsters into the conversation and just generally acting naturally. The case study in Chapter 8 illustrates how staff, working collaboratively, coped with the varied demands present within that working environment. If, for example, a potentially tense situation was developing between a member of staff and a youngster, then the other adult would subtly intervene, helping to diffuse the situation before it escalated. The collaborative approach additionally assisted that adult in assessing her own contribution to the learning context; ironically she could have been the 'problem' and not the youngster who was logically reacting to that adult's problem behaviour!

Within the wider community there are numerous people who can offer valuable input into the curriculum. Some schools do now have extensive links with industry. Additionally we have to evaluate whether we really do effectively deploy existing personnel within the school: maintenance, administrative staff colleagues, they are all valuable resource supports.

This co-operative approach to learning could facilitate a much more flexible way of grouping youngsters. One school encouraged integrated teaching across all departments in all years. In a year group of 180 students taught by six staff, one member of the humanities staff presented a key lesson to 100 youngsters whilst the other five staff took smaller groups and engaged in a variety of learning approaches. Include teaching personnel from the external community and student groupings take on even more flexibility, as do the boundaries of co-operative teaching. Such flexibility has a greater potential for meeting pupils' developmental and staffs' professional development needs than is likely within traditional structures.

Material resources

It is acknowledged that there is a paucity of material resources in schools which does influence the quality of the learning environment. There are some schools however which continually use 'lack of resources' as a reason for curriculum underfunctioning. We need to widen our concept of resources by looking at facilities in the wider community whilst simultaneously assessing our use of resources within the school.

It might well be that our segmented approach to curriculum organisation militates against the co-operative and effective use of current resources. We package material resources within defined school areas when they could be effectively used across the curriculum. Examples of cross-curricular resources are given in Chapter 9 of this book.

There has been a rapid growth in the availability of materials which can be used for the 14–19 curriculum. Teachers have to be encouraged to share evaluative thoughts about the effectiveness of materials and resources.

The students

Within the process of curriculum design, development and evaluation there has to be an awareness of the consumer group who will participate in this curriculum. An initial analysis has to be made of the developing needs of the students, so that the curriculum response is adequate to their distinct needs. Students are a crucial curriculum resource. By involving them actively in learning processes they positively shape the educative climate.

Community

Within schools we regularly work from the premise that external demands shape and dictate curriculum development. Our focus has to be redirected towards facets of the community which have much to offer to an evolutionary curriculum. These include parents, employers, voluntary agencies, commerce, the list is endless. There is a wealth of experience which can be drawn upon within the community. Simultaneously there is much that the school can give to the community through student and teacher active participation.

INSET support

The organisation and delivery of INSET is in a state of transition. Grant-related in-service training (GRIST), whilst bringing with it an administrative nightmare for local education authorities, higher education and schools, also heralds exciting developments in in-service support.

Local education authorities are now asking schools to devise their own projected staff development plans. Within these plans schools should be able to identify distinct staff development areas which can be responded to within the school situation, but with outside support.

The combined introduction of GRIST and teacher appraisal initiatives could well ensure that staff development assumes a flexibility which responds to the needs of staff. Take, for example, the theme of 'Problem-solving within the curriculum' which the school identifies as a training need. Three staff, head of house, co-ordinator of special education, head of science and technology, each attend a term's session on problem-solving offered by a training organisation over a year period.

The format of each term is organised so that two days per week are spent in school, with supporting personnel from the training establishment and the LEA developing the work within the school.

This dovetail effect of one person being released each term enables a team approach to curriculum development to be taken within the school whilst simultaneously deriving support from outside school. Additionally within a redesigned curriculum structured around a modular system of delivery it could be possible to incorporate a cohesive staff development programme within the school day.

Staff appraisal

Staff development, just as with student development, has to be accompanied by an effective programme of staff appraisal. The term 'staff appraisal' often engenders concern within the profession regarding such questions as: who does the appraisal, for what purpose and in what way? In a genuinely facilitative school, appraisal should be a key aspect of staff development.

Staff appraisal has to be mutual appraisal which involves total staff involvement. Just as counselling encourages self-exploration in both individual and group settings, so too with staff appraisal. This should allow the teacher to engage in a process of constant reassessment.

Who?

Staff appraisal could be self-directed, under the guidance and support of an external staff development facilitator. At one time the professional tutor (who, like the school counsellor, was seen to be a neutral professional) undertook staff development assessment. It could well be that such a role could be reactivated in schools or that an evolving group of personnel could assume caring responsibility for staff appraisal.

Staff at all levels regularly underfunction because they have not had the opportunity to analyse their own skills, strengths and development needs. Flexible teaching processes and patterns of student grouping enable staff to work in a more supportive learning environment which encourages staff and youngsters to co-operate in assessing and helping each other. It is possible for both staff and students to analyse the processes of learning, and to consider the diverse contributions which everyone makes to the learning environment.

Why?

Staff appraisal and development complement each other. They underpin effective curriculum design development and evaluation and in so doing shape the essential climate of learning within the school.

During a time when pupil numbers are contracting there are numerous staff in schools who feel helplessly locked into posts which they have outgrown and some teachers would welcome the opportunity to move outside the constraints and demands of their subject area.

It is conjectured that some have remained static within their distinct subject area because they have never had the opportunity to articulate their desire for change. It is assumed that the majority of staff do not want to move outside subject structures. In reality they may never have been given permission to do so.

How?

The issue of skill acquisition can only be effectively addressed as part of a caring staff development programme. As with youngsters, staff internalise learning through a process of active involvement whereby they take responsibility for their own learning in an environment of trust and support. Part 3 of this volume introduced those caring processes which should underpin 14-plus initiatives.

- flexible procedures for grouping students
- counselling approaches to learning
- problem-solving and reflective learning
- self-initiated and negotiated patterns of learning
- formative identification and assessment processes
- summative records of achievement.

These curriculum processes should lie at the heart of any caring staff development programme. Active learning involves participatory and experiential learning. This means that as a group, staff have to experience at first hand those processes of learning which underpin the pastoral response across the whole curriculum for people.

Such a strategy holds the promise of making developmental, special and professional needs more explicit than at present. It also means that such needs as are identified might be met more effectively.

STAFF DEVELOPMENT ACTIVITIES

Chapter 1

Joe

1. How could Joe's parents have been brought into early discussions about him?
2. What should the role of the head of house have been in this situation?
3. Should the teachers have come together early to discuss strategies?
4. What influence, if any, could Joe's home background have on his performance in school?
5. Could Joe's peers have positively contributed to his development?
6. How could he have become involved in a self-assessment of his needs?

Terry

1. What should the initial response of Terry's junior school have been to the psychologist's comment, 'He is finding it difficult to keep up in class'? Was such a comment helpful?
2. What liaison strategies could the junior and secondary schools have adopted to ease Terry's transition needs?
3. What do you understand by a 'structured situation' for Terry?
4. Why are some staff insecure in an environment which encourages active learning?
5. What outside agencies could the school have called upon to assist positively in responding to Terry's perceived needs?
6. How might the home have become involved?

Sarah

1. How might the school have liaised more effectively with Sarah's parents?
2. Sarah's internal reports appeared exemplary. How adequate were these reports?
3. What advice could the school have given before Sarah stayed on in the sixth form?
4. How might the support of her peers have been drawn upon to help Sarah identify some of her needs?
5. What study skills should Sarah have been offered?

6.   How could she have been extended socially?

Barry

1.   Barry compensated for his 'handicap' by being very outgoing, particularly through the medium of drama. How could his head of year and head of drama department have supported him through this developmental stage?
2.   How might the simultaneous development of Barry's peers have been enhanced through supportive group work?
3.   What are some of the possible messages which Barry was attempting to convey through his 'punk' appearance?
4.   If one aspect of any personal development curriculum is to focus upon developmental issues, how could the topic of homosexuality be sensitively addressed within the curriculum?
5.   Imagine you are a form tutor. What initial steps could you have taken to facilitate Barry's positive sexual development?

Jim

1.   How might the upper-school curriculum be so organised that all youngsters have an equal chance of full participation in that curriculum?
2.   What are your feelings about option choices? Is it possible to design an option form which allows as much freedom of choice as possible, for all youngsters?
3.   Should staff, knowing that a youngster will 'fail' a course, allow the individual to pursue such a course of study? What are some of the difficulties which staff encounter and how can they be resolved when faced with a student in this position? What implications are there for option choice structuring?
4.   In a modular curriculum form would Jim have had a more equitable curriculum option choice?
5.   Is work experience an unrealistic experience in a world of potential unemployment?
6.   How should the school prepare youngsters for and consolidate upon community experience?
7.   In what ways could schools approach the topic of education for unemployment?

Joe, Terry, Sarah, Barry and Jim and aspects of Achievement

Take each of the five case studies:

Joe   – a confirmation of role
Terry – a disruptive youngster
Sarah – an emotionally and socially underdeveloped, but academically able school leaver
Barry – sexual identity and adolescence
Jim   – a cognitively less able pupil.

Under each of ILEA's four aspects of achievement try to place yourself in the young person's situation. Indicate some of the questions and comments which you think each of these youngsters mght raise in relation to their own developmental needs. Discuss these responses and try to indicate what implications they have for upper-school curricula development.

1. What are some of the difficulties which would face teachers in the classroom when they attempt to listen and respond to many of the needs which are articulated by pupils?
2. What are some of the different perspectives which you think employers, parents and higher-education personnel may hold in connection with their views about the 'most appropriate' curriculum for youngsters with special educational needs?
3. What are some of the salient issues which do influence the climate of the school? List these in order of importance.
4. Why do you think that the needs of many youngsters with special educational needs have not been met within some upper-school curricula? Analyse the curriculum emphasis within your own school. Focus upon:

   - organisation
   - content
   - processes of learning
   - assessment.

   Assess the effectiveness of your curriculum as a positive response to special educational needs.
5. Teachers and schools can seriously destroy a youngster's level of motivation through a variety of responses. Think of a situation in your own school where this process has occurred.
6. Why is it sometimes difficult for a youngster and/or a teacher to accept failure in a group situation? Does the question of ownership of failure have to be considered?

Chapter 2

1. Refer to your own situation either as a pupil, parent or teacher. Recount whether you have been, or still are, involved in any of the three processes of pastoral care

introduced in this chapter. Critically evaluate their effectiveness as a caring response to youngsters with special educational needs.

2. From your own observations, is the role ascription of the 'disciplinary head of pastoral unit' implicit in processes 1 and 2, often designated to male members of staff?

3. What are some of the demands made upon heads of pastoral units in a school where 'standards' are apparently falling?

4. Focus upon either one of the case studies discussed in Chapter 1, or a youngster known to you and discuss how s/he could be upported by one of these processes of pastoral care.

5. Take the fourth aspect of achievement presented in Chapter 1 and try to evaluate the effectiveness of support which one of the processes of pastoral care could give to a youngster who is trying to attain this level of achievement.

6. What are some of the inherent dangers in a pastoral process which works from a premise of understanding and forgiving all?

Chapter 3

1. How is pastoral care in your school organised on a day-to-day basis? Consider such issues as:

    (i) links with other areas, particularly distinct special educational areas

    (ii) the actual daily/weekly time slots

    (iii) the responsibility of each curriculum area for pastoral care

    (iv) pastoral curriculum components.

2. Do you think that pastoral care should be timetabled as a distinct curriculum slot?

3. What are some of the salient influences which create and retain 'an environment of facilitative care'?

4. Analyse the salient features of one pastoral-care framework known to you. Comment upon its effectiveness as a viable response to adolescent needs.

5. When we refer to the needs which emanate from achievement demands we regularly and understandably concentrate upon young people. What achievement demands do teachers have to negotiate as they attempt to respond to the needs of adolescents? What implications have these for staff development?

6. Does the 'professionalisation' of pastoral care encourage the conceptualisation of care as a segmented curricula response to needs?

7. Does pastoral care within your school assume a peripheral and/or core curriculum placement? How does its placement affect the quality of care on offer?
8. Evaluate the core entitlement aims described in Figure 3.1. How relevant are these aims as a curriculum response for youngsters with special educational needs?
9. Many subject areas are being subsumed under integrated curriculum initiatives. What are some of the advantages and disadvantages to this development?
10. *A curriculum analysis exercise* Using the curriculum analysis matrix, Figure 10.1, analyse your own 14–19 curriculum structure. Assess which of the core entitlement aims are present in this curriculum form and evalute its effectiveness as a positive response to special educational needs.

Chapter 4

Personal and social education

1. There is a view held which argues that adolescents, particularly those who are disturbed and disturbing, often need to be told what is right and wrong. Do you think that this view conflicts in any way with the underlying tenets of moral education?
2. 'I never let myself get too close to the kids, they start to take advantage.' Does this attitude impinge in any way upon the honesty of relationships in the classroom?
3. Draft out the outline for a staff discussion paper on the design and development of a personal and social development programme. Give aims, objectives, resources and intended processes of learning. Design the paper so that you will be able to use it as a discussion resource for staff/curriculum development within your secondary school.
4. 'Treatment by others during childhood and adolescence is the greatest formulative influence on an adolescent's style of life.' If a child has been damaged and unloved, how can the curriculum start to make an adequate response to that child's needs?
5. 'Moral behaviour is not simply a matter of accepting social norms, it involves making personal decisions in conflict with norms.' What implications has this for the teacher involved in this style of learning, particularly when teaching those youngsters who are regularly outside the 'norms' of the prevailing school climate and the wider community?
6. Using the case study of Sarah in Chapter 1 try to assess how this process of learning would help her developmental progress.

Figure 10.1 *Curriculum analysis matrix*

Core curriculum entitlement aims:
Tick the appropriate boxes if you think that a core entitlement aim is present in a curriculum segment.
Note: In most curricula the structure will be composed of either:

i *Subjects*, e.g. mathematics, science, RE

ii *Modules*, e.g.'Man in his environment', 'The art of communication'

iii *Faculties*, e.g. creative arts, humanities

iv *Pastoral care components*, e.g. vocation preparation, study skills

There could be a combination of forms in some curriculum structures.

CURRICULUM SEGMENTS *(subjects, modules, faculties, pastoral care, etc.)*

	EXAMPLES	MATHS	SCIENCE		

Core entitlement aims (FEU, April 1985)

ADAPTABILITY					
ROLE TRANSITION					
PHYSICAL SKILLS					
INTERPERSONAL SKILLS					
VALUES					
COMMUNICATION/NUMERACY					
PROBLEM-SOLVING					
INFORMATION TECHNOLOGY					
SOCIETY					
LEARNING SKILLS					
HEALTH EDUCATION					
CREATIVITY					
ENVIRONMENT					
SCIENCE AND TECHNOLOGY					
COPING					

7. The case study of Barry illustrated that he had accepted himself and his sexual identity. How do you think personal and social development may have helped others in the group to look at issues which relate to self-acceptance and tolerance?

8. It is argued that a number of very sensitive topics currently being introduced into personal and social education

curricula should not be the remit of the school curriculum. What are your views on this?

Vocational and pre-vocational education

1. Is vocational education in your school an 'enabling curriculum response' to the needs of the school leaver?
2. How does experiential learning encourage a youngster to experience success in those achievement aspects introduced in Chapter 1?
3. How could the school become involved in the wider community, as part of the vocational experience?
4. Consider Watts' conclusions about why some schools feel unable to address the issues of unemployment. Do some of his conclusions ring true within the school situation?
5. Consider the question of unemployment as a curriculum theme.

    (a) Should the school become actively involved in preparing young people for possible unemployment?
    (b) Analyse the comments of both young people and parents. What is your response, as a teacher, to some of these comments?

6. Prepare a curriculum development document for your school which is going to contribute to the formulation of a school policy on vocational education and address the issue of unemployment arguing for:

    (a) its inclusion or
    (b) its omission within the curriculum.

    Consider the school and community situation in which this curriculum component is going to be developed.
7. Will the development of tertiary education encourage the emergence of an entitlement curriculum for all students in post-16 education?
8. Focus upon a particular special school or FE college known to you; describe and analyse the leavers' programme within that school or the special needs programme within that college.

Study skills

1. List some of the key learning skills which a young person needs to enable her to participate actively in the learning process.

2. Describe and evaluate your own experiences as a student. Were you (are you) equipped to effectively negotiate the demands placed upon you?
3. (a) List some of the study demands which you have or have had to cope with as a student.
   (b) List some of the skills which supported you in this process.
   (c) List some of the skills which you did not have, which would have helped you in this process.
4. In what ways can the home help in supporting the study needs of youngsters? How can homes militate against the creation of effective learning patterns?
5. Do you think that the so-called academically less able adolescent needs a different repertoire of study skills?
6. What are some of the processes which academically able youngsters can engage in to conceal inadequate learning skills?
7. Refer to your school curriculum. Does it include study skills as a curriculum component?
8. Take one of the core study skill issues. Prepare a work sheet which could be used as a curriculum resource example to meet this particular study demand.

Chapter 5

The role of the tutor

1. Indicate some of the key tasks and procedures which you think should be part of the tutorial role.

As tutor
2. What perceptions do the following people hold of your role? (Attempt to organise your responses around some of the tasks which they expect you to perform.)
   head teacher
   head of pastoral unit
   subject staff
   special needs staff
   parents
   students
3. Which of Marland's three tutorial types (Figure 5.1) operates in your school? Comment upon its effectiveness as a positive response to special educational needs.
4. How much initial information are you given about youngsters in your tutorial group who have special educational needs?

5. 'Effective tutoring is good teaching'. Comment upon this in connection with the relationship between the pastoral and the mainstream curriculum.
6. Should you be the first line of referral for youngsters in your group who may be experiencing difficulties in the mainstream curriculum?

As a head of pastoral unit
7. How do mainstream staff interpret your role? (Attempt to organise your responses around some of the task expectations associated with the role.)
8. How do staff interpret the pastoral response:

    ·(i)   as a punitive agency?
    (ii)   as a welfare agency?
    (iii)   as a curriculum aspect which complements and supports the wider curriculum?
    (iv)   any other view?

9. Who should be the first line of referral for youngsters with difficulties, yourself or the tutor?

As mainstream staff
10. What are the key tasks and procedures implicit in

    ●   the head-of-pastoral-unit role?
    ●   the tutor role?

11. If a youngster becomes disruptive in your lesson, who would be your first line of referral?

As a head of department
12. If a number of your staff report that a youngster is having learning difficulties and/or is exhibiting disruptive patterns of behaviour, who should be his first line of referral?
13. How much information are you given about young people with special needs who will be taught in your department?
14. Consider the three personnel roles of a class teacher, a tutor, a special educator. What management and curriculum procedures would be necessary to facilitate a whole-school approach to the pastoral care of youngsters with special needs?
15. What do you understand by the term 'discipline'? Is there a difference between discipline and obedience?
16. Take the three structural views of tutorial organisation and consider the strengths and weaknesses of these environments

as a response to the learning needs of youngsters who are (i) isolated and underachieving; (ii) disruptive and immature.

passive structure
- (i) isolated and underachieving
- (ii) disruptive and immature

laissez-faire *structure*
- (i) isolated and underachieving
- (ii) disruptive and immature

active structure
- (i) isolated and underachieving
- (ii) disruptive and immature

17. In a secondary school known to you:
- (i) assess the immediate appeal of the aesthetic environment
- (ii) try to observe a selection of learning bases and comment upon their aesthetic environment. Assess how these surroundings contribute to the prevailing discipline ethos.

18. The following comments have been made by a group of secondary school staff about mixed ability teaching. This is an issue which regularly raises concern amongst staff.

> 'We supposedly in our school teach mixed ability ... but nobody really does'. (PE teacher)

> 'Who trains us to teach mixed ability?' (Remedial teacher)

> 'How can you teach mixed ability to 36 kids?' (Head of First Year)

> 'I'm supposed to be getting them through an exam syllabus, with set standards, expressed through set questions which demand set answers. You tell me how I'm supposed to prepare them for this within a group of kids which has some who can hardly read.' (History teacher)

> 'Within my so called mixed ability group I have kids who don't want to learn affecting those who do. How do you justify that?' (Domestic Science teacher)

> 'In my mixed ability I just teach that bulk of pupils in the middle, it's called mediocracy.' (Head of Maths)

'The school adheres to a policy of mixed ability ... but yes, we do "set", particularly with academic subjects. Streaming? I prefer to call it "setting for ability".' (Headteacher).

'Mr Jones prides himself on running a mixed ability class but he has the "bright" kids in a row in front of him. The conforming "less able" to one side, the conforming "average" group on the other, and the disruptive lot mess about at the back.' (Probationer)

Mixed ability teaching is a structural form which encourages the flexible grouping of youngsters and facilitates an effective teaching response to a wide range of educational needs. Focus upon your own school and consider the following issues:

- What do you understand by the term mixed ability teaching?
- Write six sentences giving the pros and cons of this process of working.
- Make a list of the facilitative forces in school which encourage mixed ability grouping.
- Make a list of the restrictive forces.
- Balance these items against each other.
- Analyse how realistically restrictive the forces in the list are. Are there any ways in which the staff could overcome these? Mixed ability or flexible grouping places a number of demands upon the organisational skills of the educator. Make two lists under the headings below itemising:

- the tasks inherent in this form of grouping
- the skills which you as a group manager will need to help you successfully carry out this form of tutoring/teaching.

  organisational tasks   *implementation and maintenance skills*

Isolate at least three priority skills which you feel staff in your school would need to develop in training sessions for mixed ability teaching.

  (i)
  (ii)
  (iii)

Chapter 6

1. What do you understand by the term 'counselling' in the school situation?

2. How could the counselling response support young people as they negotiate the adolescent demands expounded upon by Erikson (1968) and Hargreaves (1984)?
3. Consider the qualities of congruence, unconditional positive regard and empathetic understanding. How should they influence the learning relationship within the classroom?
4. Comment upon those para-counselling skills and assess their effectiveness in helping the teacher respond adequately to adolescent needs.
5. Through negotiation with one of your students mutually develop a contract which will enable her to achieve an element of success effectively.
6. In a group situation encourage a youngster to identify a problem and then to work upon a plan of action, with the support of significant others within the group, to tackle that problem.

Chapter 7

1. Isolate those forms of identification and assessment which are prevalent in your school situation. Comment upon their effectiveness as initial indicators of special educational needs.
2. What are some of the inherent difficulties present within those formative methods observed, for example, in GCSE courses?
3. List some of those advantages and disadvantages of self and peer assessment within the group situation.
4. 'Formative assessment cannot help but be subjective and very hit and miss.' Is this a fair comment from a science teacher who is coping with an all-ability teaching group?
5. What implications have formative assessment procedures for the ways in which the teacher organises the learning environment?
6. Summative records of achievement are a collation of a student's developing achievement. Do they have as much credibility as traditional examination forms?

Resources for staff development: 14–18 curriculum

Hargreaves, D. (1982)   *The Challenge for the Comprehensive School*
                         London: Routledge & Kegan Paul
Hargreaves questions the prevailing view of the concept of comprehensivisation. Given the changing demands upon schools, we have to analyse how we structure curriculum

experiences. The results of this analysis could well mean redefining teaching roles within schools.

Hargreaves, D. (1984)   *Improving Secondary Schools*
London: ILEA
A report of a committee which analysed the curriculum and organisation of secondary schools. The salient focus of this report was that it stressed four key achievement aspects within which youngsters are developing. The report introduces those curriculum responses (some of which are the subject of this volume), regarded as a necessary prerequisite for positive learning development amongst adolescents.

Reynolds, D. (ed.)   (1985)   *Studying School Effectiveness*
London: Falmer
A selection of papers covering a wide range of issues which underpin current deliberations on 14–19 education. For example, the school climate, pastoral care, examinations, institutional developments. Whilst the book is theoretically focused, the practising teacher should be able to relate some of this theory to 'out there, in the classroom'.

Sayer, J. (1985)   *What Future for Secondary Schools?*
London: Falmer
A provocative volume which encourages the reader to question the reasons why we have schools. The first section looks at difficulties which the secondary teacher has to face, the second offers radical proposals for future developments. Some of the issues raised in this volume succinctly link with issues which Sayer raises in the introductory volume to the *Special Needs in Ordinary Schools* Series.

Sayer, J. (1987)   *Secondary Schools for All?*
London: Cassell
A challenging exploration of management issues within the secondary curriculum, assessing their effect upon special education in its widest sense.

Staff development issues

Day, C. and Moore, R. (eds) (1986)   *Staff Development in the Secondary School*
London: Croom Helm
Staff development observed from a school management perspective. Key issues in the management of schools are considered. Amongst them are: the training and development needs of

managers; how heads and deputies use their time; counselling and performance appraisal; problems in staff development; action research; working with industry.

Dunham, J. (1984)   *Stress in Teaching*
                    London: Croom Helm
Dunham discusses the continual stresses and strains which teachers have to contend with. For example, organisational changes, role conflict, pressures of pupil behaviour, poor working conditions, pressures on layers of management. The first section considers these stresses, the second looks at positive responses to help teachers cope with these pressures.

Further Education Unit/Department of   *From Coping to Confidence*
Education and Science (1985)   Slough: NFER
A versatile staff developoment resource. Although designed initially for staff in FE, the curriculum processes which are explored transcend organisational boundaries. The pack contains six modules: Setting the Scene; Developing the Curriculum; The Curriculum in Action; Strategies for Teaching and Learning; Promoting Self Reliance; Monitoring Student Progress and Achievement. The modules are accompanied by a user's guide and a provocative and illuminating eight-programme video which develops the process issues raised in the modules. It is a well-organised and relevant development pack.

Further Education Unit (1986/7)   *Planning Staff Development*
                                 London: HMSO
A series of very useful bulletins 'aimed at supporting local education authorities in the process of managing and co-ordinating authority wide schemes of staff development and INSET in response to new specific grant arrangements for in-service training of teachers from 1987 onwards'.
The first five bulletins focus upon:

• planning and implementing LEA schemes for post-14 staff development/INSET
• approaches to staff development
• collaborative arrangements in the planning implementation of INSET/staff development
• planning staff replacement
• special educational needs.

They present a succinct introduction to current issues of staff development.

Kirsta, A. (1986)   *The Book of Stress Survival*
London: Unwin
A useful programme for coping with stress, organised in four parts: analysing stress; preventing stress; ways to relax; high stress situations. A number of these exercises could be profitably used in developmental group work with staff.

Main, A. (1985)   *Educational Staff Development*
London: Croom Helm
An attempt to get behind the concept of staff development through an analysis of a range of staff development models. The conclusive outcome of this analysis is to focus upon the teacher as the learner who requires a supportive, facilitative learning environment in which personal and professional skills can be effectively developed.

McMahon, A. *et al.* (1984)   *Guidelines for Review and Internal Development in Schools*
Harlow: Longman for SCDC
A description of a joint project (Schools Curriculum Development Committee/Bristol University) which explores strategies for assisting staff across the whole-school to self-review curriculum policy and practice. The GRIDS process of self-evaluation follows five stages: Getting Started; Initial Review/s; Action for Development; Overview and Restart. It is a process of review which links with those teacher/school evaluation and appraisal processes raised in this chapter and introduced by HMI (DES).

Oldroyd, D. *et al.* (1984)   *School Based Staff Staff Development*
Harlow: Longmans (for Schools Council)
Eleven schools in Avon are used as models for good staff development practice. A wide range of relevant training and development activities are given. For example, the organisation of a whole-staff conference identifying staff development needs, school-based remedial INSET work. An invaluable practical resource which has been tried and tested in the classroom.

Paisey, A. (ed.) (1983)   *The Effective Teacher*
London: Ward Lock
A range of contributors consider the theme of effectiveness within the teaching profession from a number of perspectives. Among them: the purpose of schooling; knowing the law; understanding organisation and management; exercising leadership; developing a personal career; monitoring personal health.

Paisey, A. (1984)   *School Management: A Case Approach*
      London: Harper Educational
A diverse range of management themes are considered, taken
from thirty school case studies. Among the issues raised are: staff
development; pupil grouping; teaching methods and techniques;
relations with parents; financial management; restructuring the
school. Introduces the concept and practice of management to a
whole-staff spectrum.

Group structuring/classroom observation

Department of Education and Science Teacher Education Project,
(1976–81)

Brown, G. and Hatton, N. (1982)   *Explanations and Explaining*
      London: Macmillan
Kerry, T. (1981)   *Teaching Bright Pupils*
      London: Macmillan
Kerry, T. (1982)   *Effective Questioning*
      London: Macmillan
Kerry, T. and Sands, M. (1982)   *Handling Classroom Groups*
      London: Macmillan
Kerry, T. and Sands, M. (1982)   *Mixed Ability Teaching*
      London: Macmillan
Wragg, T. (1981)   *Class Management and Control*
      London: Macmillan.
These volumes form part of the teacher education project
financed by the DES to improve initial and in-service training.
They are provocative training books which encourage the reader
to develop some of the topics raised, in the classroom setting.
They stress the importance of professionals working collabora-
tively: 'An open profession permits people to co-operate to hone
professional skills, and to share both insights and problems'.
Consequently one part of each work book contains exercises
which encourage co-operative staff development. Attractively
presented booklets which are practical and in touch with the
realities of classroom life.

Docking, J. W. (1980)   *Control and Discipline in Schools*
      London: Harper & Row
An analysis of theoretical and practical issues which underpin the
structured learning environment. Among the issues considered
are: the concept of discipline; definitions of misbehaviour;
external and internal influences upon behaviour; teacher/pupil

relationships; classroom management skills; the curriculum; pastoral care and special provision; punishment. This is a very readable text. Extensive reference is made to classroom research which gives it added potency.

Robertson, J. (1981)   *Effective Classroom Control*
London: Hodder & Stoughton
Offers sound and practical advice to the teacher in the classroom. Covers such issues as: communicating authority; conveying enthusiasm; analysing unwanted behaviour; dealing with unwanted behaviour. Concludes with a very useful 'Checklist for Successful Teaching' which summarises seven key requirements for effective classroom control.

Skinner, A. *et al.* (1983)   *Disaffection from School*
London: National Youth Bureau
An annotated bibliography and literature review. A comprehensive and succinct resource book which analyses reasons for disaffection and the responses of the school to this issue.

Stubbs, M. and Delamont, S. (1976)   *Explorations in Classroom Observation*
Chichester: Wiley
An excellent, highly relevant collection of papers on classroom research. This quote from the Preface sums up its focus: 'There is something radically wrong with educational research. Few teachers read it. Planning ignores it ... Events in classrooms *are* complex. The papers in this book explore precisely that complexity.'

Upton, G and Gobell, A. (1980)   *Behaviour Problems in the Comprehensive School*
University College (Cardiff)
Faculty of Education.
A comprehensive volume containing a range of papers grouped under four sections: basic considerations – the nature of misbehaviour; classroom life; current practice; wider perspectives. Each paper is accompanied by a useful bibliography.

Wragg, E. (ed). (1984)   *Classroom Teaching Skills*
Croom Helm
A selection of papers which report the research findings of the DES-funded Teacher Education Project. A succinct analysis of classroom case studies based upon comparative classroom environments.

Pastoral care

Hamblin, D. (1984) *Pastoral Care–A Training Manual*
Oxford: Blackwell
A comprehensive volume which covers a range of issues including skill training and management implications for effective pastoral care.

Hamblin, D. (1986) *A Pastoral Programme*
Oxford: Blackwell
Mindful of the need to avoid a package approach to pastoral care, the volume does however offer a pastoral programme for secondary schools. The emphasis is upon 'programme' and not necessarily upon the wider concept of a pastoral curriculum which impinges upon all activity within the school. The second part of the book contains a wide range of activities which can be used in the tutorial environment.

Miller, J. (1982) *Tutoring*
London: HMSO.
A staff development training manual which focuses upon the guidance and counselling role of the tutor in vocational preparation. Analyses the skills, tasks and settings of tutorial activity. Contains a perceptive 'Tutorial Development Programme' checklist which, although addressed to the college situation, can be easily adapted to the school environment.

Counselling and developmental group work

Button, L. (1974) *Developmental Group Work with Adolescents*
London: Hodder & Stoughton
A very practical book which focuses upon adolescent development within group settings. A range of pertinent techniques are given which the teacher can usefully draw upon in the classroom.

Galloway, D. (1981) *Teaching and Counselling*
Harlow: Longman
A clearly-organised book. Eighteen pairs of case studies (nine each for primary and secondary school) are given. Each pair contains a contextual consideration of a school followed by the case history of a youngster who attends that school. Themes are introduced at the beginning of the case study and questions follow issues raised in each study. A thought-provoking staff development text.

Inskipp, F. and Johns, H. (1980)   *Principles of Counselling I and II*
                                        Alexia Publications: St Leonards-
                                        on-Sea.
Two sets of audio tapes which explore the basic counselling
principles underlying the three-stage counselling model introduced in Chapter 6.
The companion volume, *A Manual for Trainers*, develops issues
raised in the tapes and is a resource book for running basic
counselling courses.

Jones, A. (1984)   *Counselling Adolescents – School and After*
(2nd edn)   London: Kogan Page
A text which defines counselling and then emphasises three skills
and personal qualities necessary for counselling to be effectively
delivered, both in individual and group settings, with youngsters
and staff.

Nelson-Jones, R. (1986)   *Human Relationship Skills*
                          London: Cassell
A comprehensive theoretical introduction to relationship skills.
Through the inclusion of detailed training exercises, it encourages
the reader to apply theoretical considerations to practical situations.

Rogers, C. (1961)   *On Becoming a Person*
                    London: Constable
Rogers, C. (1983)   *Freedom to Learn for the 80s*
                    London: Charles Merrill
Two books which discuss the process of developmental growth.
The process of 'becoming a person' involves the individual
engaging in positive relationships. For the teacher in the
classroom the realisation of positive and honest relationships
with students involves risk-taking. It also develops from a
baseline of trust whereby the teacher is able to stand aside from
role performances and in so doing engages in essentially honest
relationships with youngsters.

Vocational education

Hayes, J. and Nutman, P. (1981)   *Understanding the Unemployed*
                                  London: Tavistock
An exploration of the psychosocial consequences of unemployment. 'The purpose of this book is to enhance the understanding
of these professionals (helping professions) of the possible
consequences that unemployment has for the individual.' A
provocative text which should be essential reading for those staff
engaged in the processes of vocational preparation.

Roberts, K. (1984)   *School Leavers and their Prospects*
                Milton Keynes: Open University
A very realistic text which grapples honestly with a number of issues now facing school leavers. A critical analysis is made of government responses to the situation.

Watts, A. G. (1983)   *Education, Unemployment and the Future of Work*
                Milton Keynes: Open University
As well as tackling the salient implications of unemployment for the school leaver, consideration is made of a range of viable positive responses to the demands of unemployment for youngsters. One curriculum response model is given which, under seven curricula objectives, analyses the skills which a youngster needs in order to retain a degree of positive self-worth in a growing situation of unemployment.

Records of achievement

Balogh, J. (1982)   *Profile Reports for School-leavers*
                Harlow: Longman (for Schools Council)
An assessment of a range of methods which are used by schools to record the evaluative experiences of youngsters. Useful ideas and practical suggestions are given for profile development.

Broadfoot, P. (ed). (1986)   *Profiles and Records of Achievement*
                London: Cassell
A wide range of papers are presented which condense the experience of professionals who have been involved in developing and implementing profiles and records-of-achievement schemes.

Goacher, B. (1983)   *Recording Achievement at 16+*
                Harlow: Longman (for Schools Council)
A description of the attempts of twenty-one schools to develop more effective recording procedures for youngsters. Honest account is given of the experiences of both the pilot co-ordinator and the participating schools when involved in the process of curriculum innovation.

Bibliography

Additional annotated bibliographies of books which can be used in both the curriculum and staff development activities are given in Chapters 9 and 10 respectively.

Balogh, P. (1982) *Profile Reports for School Leavers*. Harlow: Longman (for Schools Council).

Best, R., Jarvis, C. and Ribbens, (eds) (1980) *Perspectives on Pastoral Care*. London: Heinemann.

Brennan, N. (1979) *Curricular Needs of Slow Learners*. London: Evans/ Methuen.

Broadfoot, P. (ed.) (1986) *Profiles and Records of Achievement*. London: Cassell.

Burgess, T. and Adams, E. (1985) *Records of Achievement at 16+*. Slough: NFER/Nelson.

Button, L. (1981) *Group Tutoring for the Form Teacher*. London: Hodder & Stoughton.

Dean, J. *et al*. (1979) *The Sixth Form and Its Alternatives*. Slough: NFER.

Department of Education and Science (1973) *Education (Work Experience) Act*. London: HMSO.

Department of Education and Science (1981) *Education Act*. London: HMSO.

Department of Education and Science (1984) *Records of Achievement: A Statement of Policy*. London: HMSO.

Dewey, J. (1966) 'The Child and the Curriculum' in Golby, M. *et al*. (1975) *Curriculum Design*. Milton Keynes: Open University.

Egan, G. (1975) *The Skilled Helper*. Monterey, CA: Brooks/Cole.

Erikson, E. (1968) *Identity: Youth and Crisis*. London: Faber & Faber.

Fiedler, F. E. (1950) in Nelson-Jones, R. (1982) *The Theory and Practice of Counselling Psychology*. London: Cassell.

Fish, J. (1985) *Special Education: The Way Ahead*. Open University Press, quoted in Sayer, J. (1987) *Secondary Schools for All?* London: Cassell.

Further Education Unit/Department of Education and Science (1981a) *Vocational Preparation*. London: HMSO.

Further Education Unit/Department of Education and Science (1981b) *Students with special Needs in FE*. London: HMSO.

Further Education Unit/Department of Education and Science (1984) *Routes to Coping*. London: HMSO.

Further Education Unit/Department of Education and Science (1985) *Progressing to College: a 14–16 Core*. London: HMSO.

Further Education Unit/Department of Education and Science (1985) *From Coping to Confidence*. London: HMSO.

Further Education Unit/Schools Curriculum Development Committee/ Department of Education and Science (1985) *Supporting TVEI*. London: HMSO.

Galloway, D. (1981) *Teaching and Counselling*. Harlow: Longman.

Galloway, D. *et al.* (1982) *Schools and Disruptive Pupils*. Harlow: Longman.

Galloway, D. (1985) *Schools, Pupils and Special Educational Needs*. London: Croom Helm.

Gilmore, S. (1973) *The Counsellor in Training*. Prentice-Hall: New Jersey, USA.

Gipps, C. and Cross, H. (1984) *Local Education Authorities' Policies in Identification and Provision for Children with Special Educational Needs in Ordinary Schools*, Occasional Paper 3. University of London Institute of Education.

Goacher, B. (1983) *Recording Achievement at 16+*. Harlow: Longman (for Schools Council).

Goldstein, H. and Levy, P.C. (1984) 'Tests in Education'. *Sunday Times,* 5 July 1984.

Hamblin, D. (1978) *The Teacher and Pastoral Care*. Oxford: Blackwell.

Hamblin, D. (ed.) (1981) *Problems and Practice of Pastoral Care*. Oxford: Blackwell.

Hamblin, D. (1981) *Teaching Study Skills*. Oxford: Blackwell.

Hargreaves, D. (1972) *Inter-personal Relations and Education*. London: Routledge & Kegan Paul.

Hargreaves, D. (1982) *The Challenge for the Comprehensive School*. London: Routledge & Kegan Paul.

Hargreaves Report (1984) *Improving Secondary Schools*. London: ILEA.

Hegarty, S. and Pocklington, K. (1981) *Educating Pupils with Special Needs in the Ordinary School*. Windsor: NFER.

HMI (1979) *A View of Curriculum*. London: HMSO.

HMI (1983) *Curriculum 11–16: 'Towards a Statement of Entitlement'*. London: HMSO.

HMI (1985) *Quality in Schools: Evaluation and Appraisal*. London: HMSO.

Joint Board for Pre-Vocational Education (1985) *The Certificate of Pre-Vocational Education*. BTEC and CGLI.

Laslett, R. (1977) *Educating Maladjusted Children*. London: Granada.

McPhail, P. (1972) *In Other People's Shoes*. Harlow: Longman.

Mansell, J. (1985) In Joint Board for Pre-Vocational Education – *The Certificate of pre-Vocational Education*. BTEC and CGLI.

Mansell, J. (1987) 'Reprieved Unit Hits Out Again'. *Times Educational Supplement*, 6 March 1987.

Marland, M. (1974) *Pastoral Care*. London: Heinemann.

Melia, T. (1987) 'Lack of Vocation Hampers Colleges'. *Times Higher Educational Supplement*, 6 March 1987.

Moriarty, H. (1987) 'Endangered Species – The Specialist Academic Teachers Face Extinction in the Comprehensive'. *Times Educational Supplement*, 16 March 1987.

Morton-Williams, R. *et al.* (1970) *Sixth Form Pupils and Teachers*. Vol. 1, *Books for Schools*. Schools Council Sixth Form Survey.

National Association of Head Teachers (1986) Consultative document on 14–18 education.

Paisey, A. (1981) *Organisation and Management in Schools*. Harlow: Longman.

Powell, J. (1969) *Why Am I afraid to Tell You Who I Am?* London: Fontana/Collins.

Redl, F. (1957) *The Aggressive Child*. Chicago: Chicago Free Press.

Rogers, C. (1961) *On Becoming a Person*. London: Constable.

Rogers, C. (1983) *Freedom to Learn for the 80s*. Westerville, OH: Merrill.

Sayer, J. (1987) *Secondary Schools For All?* London: Cassell.

Schools Council (1981) *The Practical Curriculum* Working Paper 70. Methuen Educational.

Spooner, R. (1979) 'Pastoral Care and the Myth of Never Ending Toil' in Galloway (1981) op. cit.

Thomas, D. (1978) *The Social Psychology of Childhood Disability*. London: Methuen & Co.

Trethowan, D. (1987) *Appraisal and Target Setting*. London: Harper & Row.

Walker, A. (1982) *Underqualified and Underemployed: Handicapped Young People in the Labour Market*. London: Macmillan.

Warnock Report (1978). London: HMSO.

Watts, A. (1978) 'Unemployment: Implications for Careers Education', *Journal of Curriculum Studies* **10** (3) pp. 233–50.

Wilensky, H. (1964) 'The Professionalisation of Everyone?', *American Journal of Sociology*, September 1964, pp. 137–58. Chicago: University of Chicago Press.

Author Index

Subject Index